Newport

C000224901

& Chepstow

Abersychan	3	New Inn	5
Bassaleg	17	Newport	19
Bettws	12	Parc-Seymour	24
Bishpool	16	Penhow	25
Blaenavon	1	Penperlleni	5
Caerleon	15	Ponthir	15
Caerwent	26	Pontnewynydd	4
Caldicot	28	Pontypool	4
Castleton	30	Portskewett	29
Celtic Lakes	18	Redwick	27
Chepstow	31	Ringland	23
Croesyceiliog	9	Rogerstone	12
Cwmbran	7	Rogiet	28
Duffryn	20	Shirenewton	26
Gaer	19	Snatchwood	3
Griffithstown	6	Somerton	21
Liswerry	21	St. Arvans	31
Llangybi	24	St. Woolos	19
Llanover	1	Stelvio	19
Llantarnam	10	Stow Park	19
Llantrisant	25	Sudbrook	29
Llanyrafon	10	Talywain	2
Magor	27	Underwood	23
Maindee	16	Undy	27
Malpas	13	Usk	30
Marshfield	30	Wainfelin	4

Streetezee®

Newport
Cwmbran, Pontypool & Chepstow

Key to street plans
Allwedd i blaniau stryd

Street plans drawn at a scale of 4 inches to 1 mile
Arluniwyd y blaniau yn ôl y raddfa 4 modfedd i 1 filltir

M4	Motorway	Traffordd
A48	A road (Trunk road)	Ffordd A (Priffordd)
B4281	B road	Ffordd B
	Through road	Ffordd drwodd
	Dual carriageway	Ffordd ddeuol
	Track/Footpath	Llwybr/Llwybr troed
	Railway	Rheilffordd
	Built up area	Ardal adeiledig
	Recreation ground	Maes chwarae
	Woods and forest	Coedtir a choedwig
✚	Health centre	Canolfan iechyd
	Petrol station	Gorsaf betrol
✠	Places of worship	Mannau addoliad
	Police station	Gorsaf heddlu
⊠	Post Office	Swyddfa'r Post
✆	Telephone	Ffon
	Toilet facility	Cyfleustra toiled
P	Car parks (major)	(prif) Maes parcio
	Caravan/camp site	Safloedd carafannau gwersyll
i	Information centre	Canolfan hysbysrwydd
	Golf Course	Maes golff
M	Museum/Theatre	Amgueddfa/Theatr
	Public house	Tafarndy
42	House numbers	Rhifau Tai

Blaenavon

Middle Coedcae

Forge Side

Talywain

Snatchwood

Pentre-Poid

Wainfelin

Varteg

Garndiffaith

Abersychan

Trevethin

Ponthewnydd

Pontypool

Llanover

Perperlleni

Little Mill

A40

A4042

B4598

B4269

A4043

B4246

A472

A449

A4810

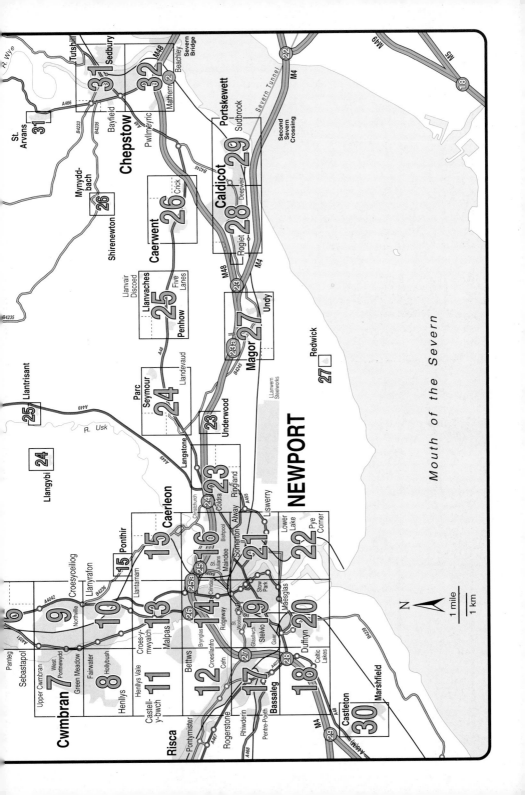

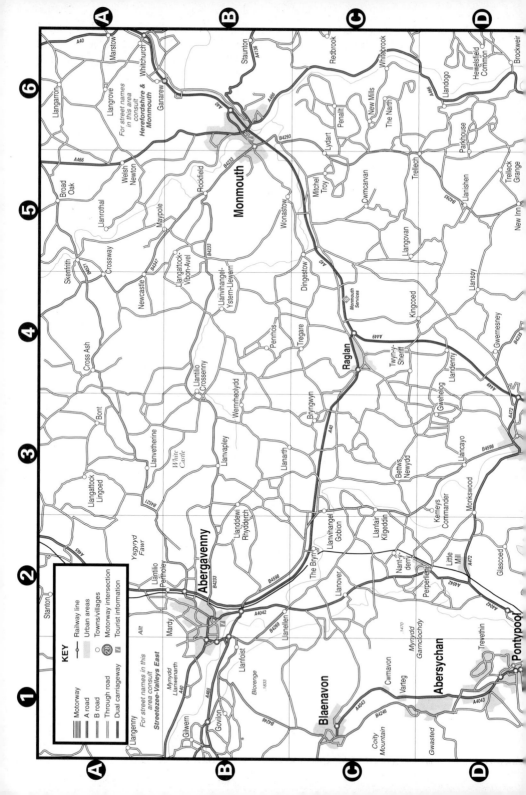

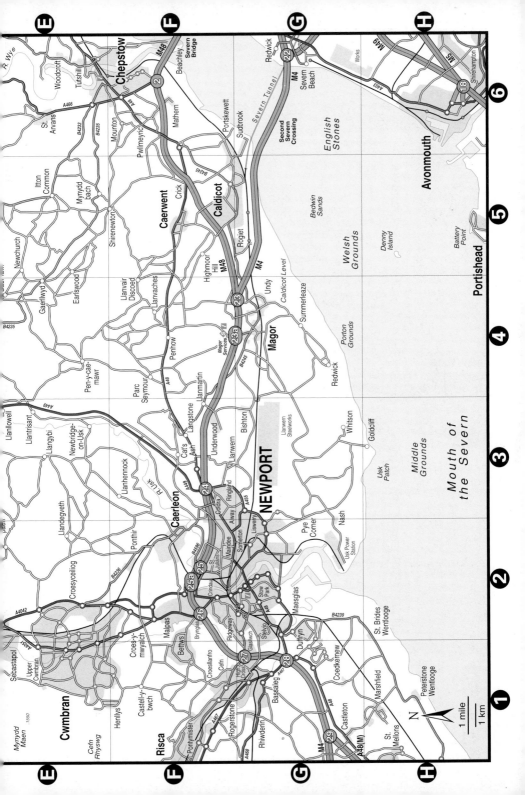

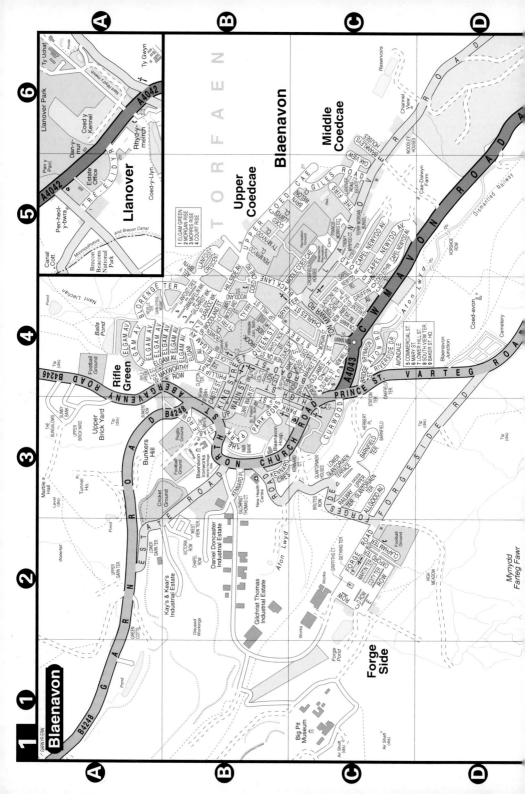

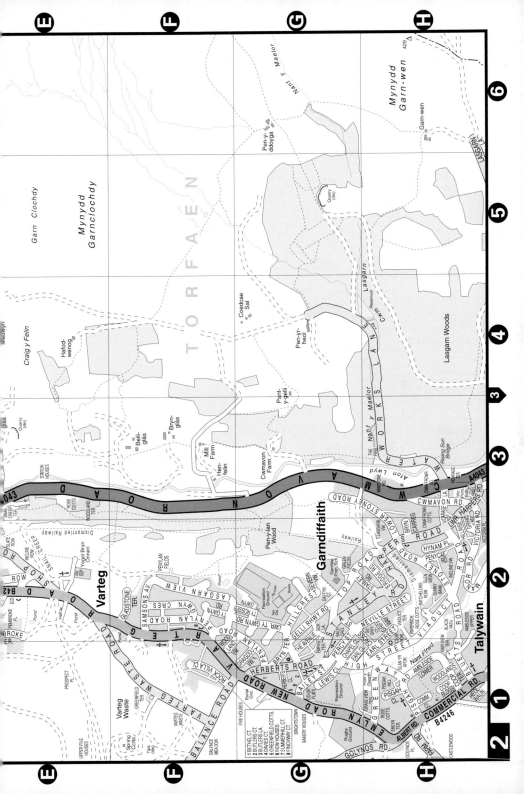

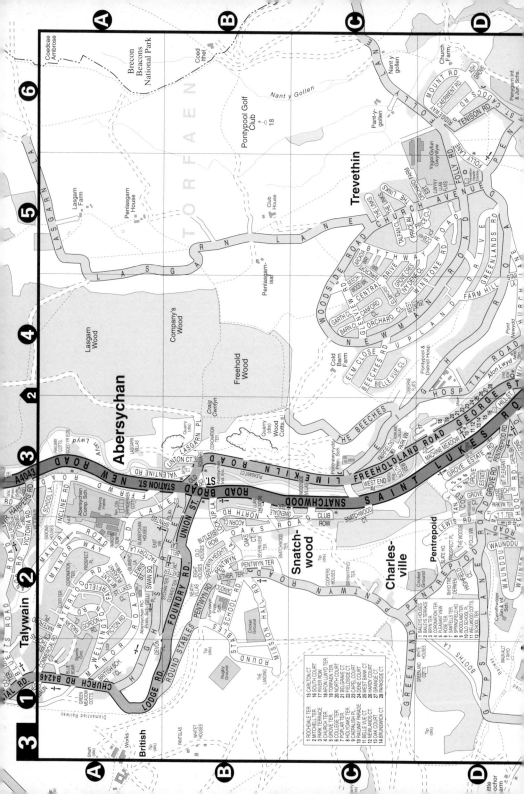

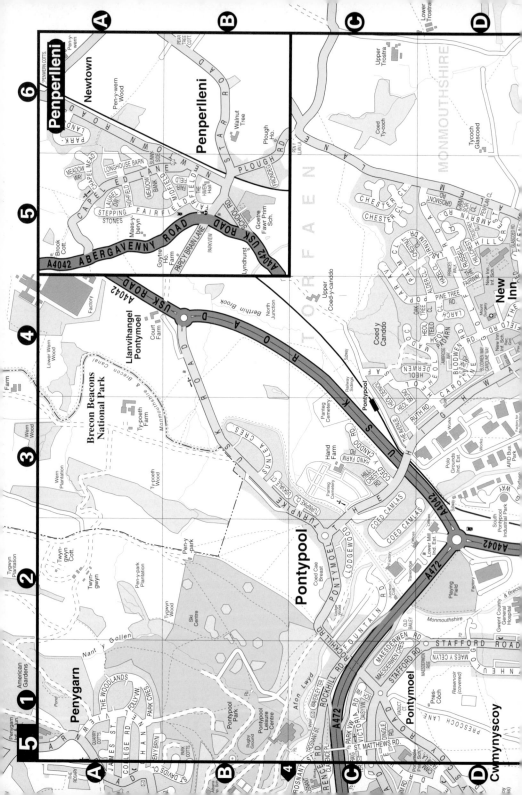

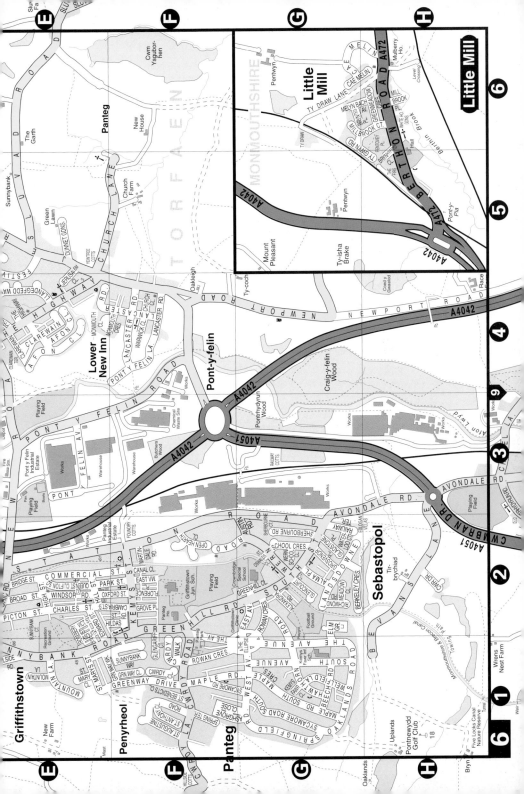

Little Mill

Griffithstown

Penyrheol

Panteg

Little Mill

Panteg

Lower New Inn

Pont-y-felin

Sebastopol

Wrens Nest Farm

Five Locks Canal Nature Reserve

Pontnewydd Golf Club

TORFAEN

MONMOUTHSHIRE

A4042

A4051

A472

NEWPORT ROAD

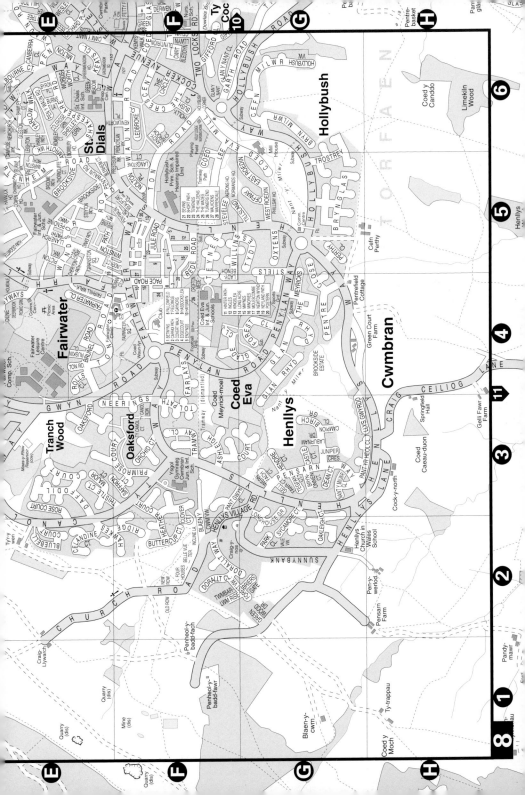

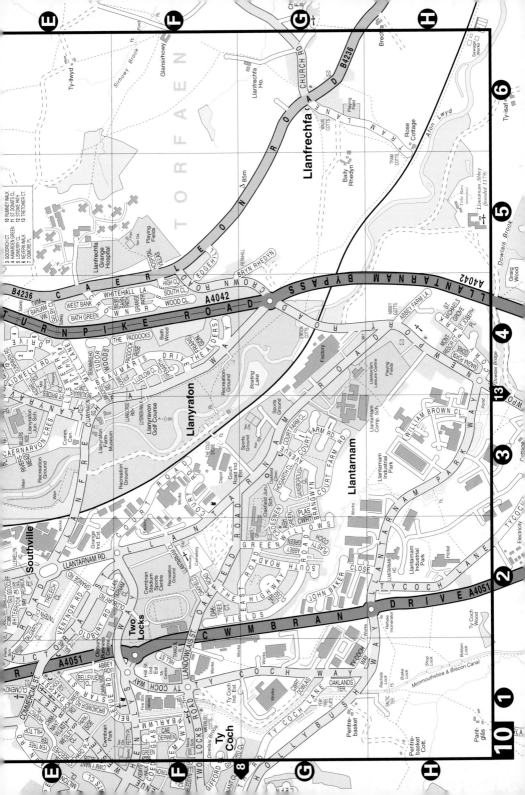

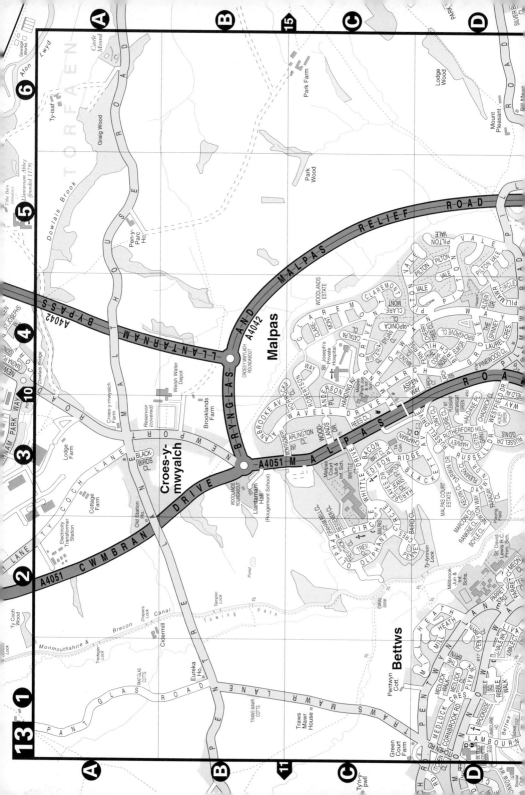

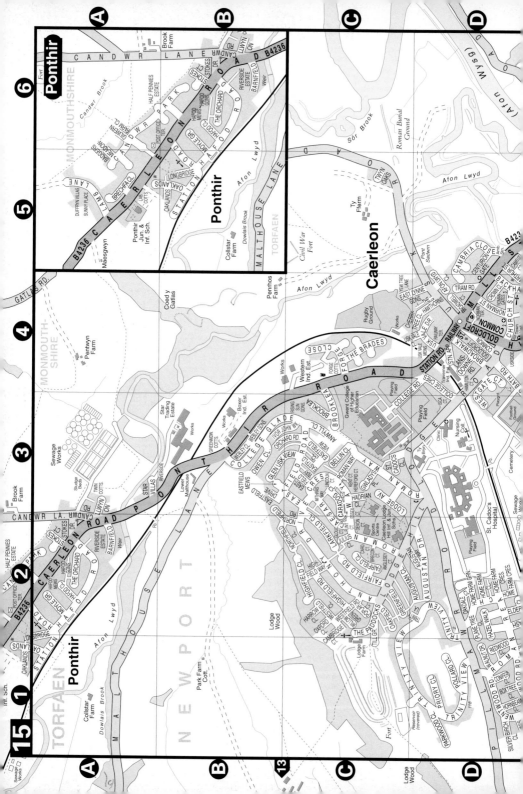

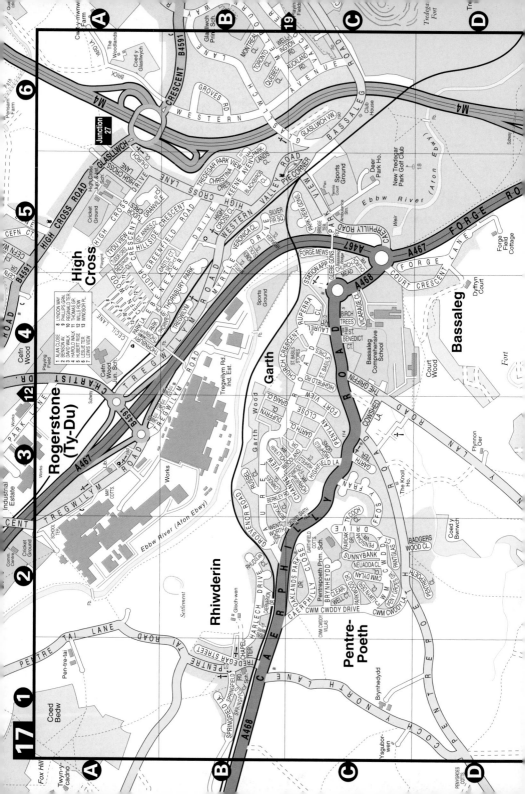

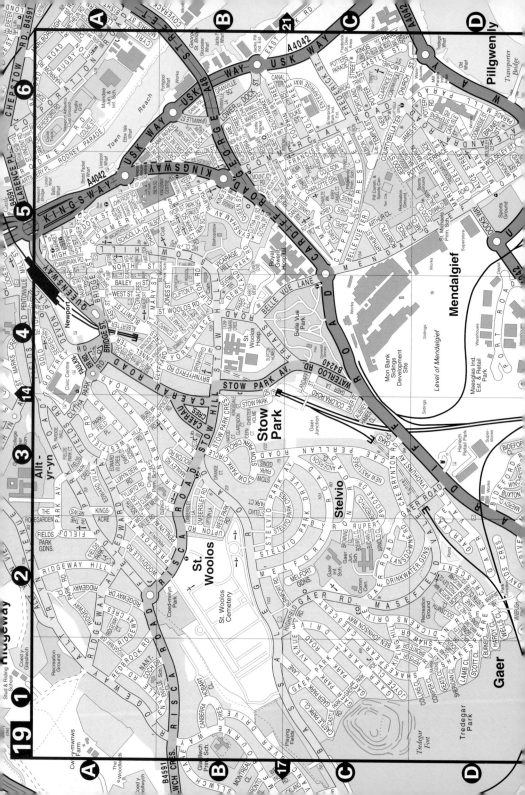

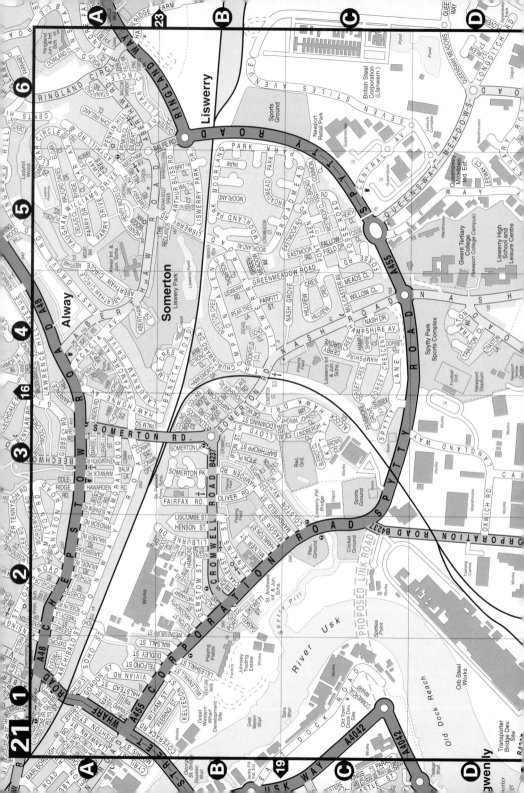

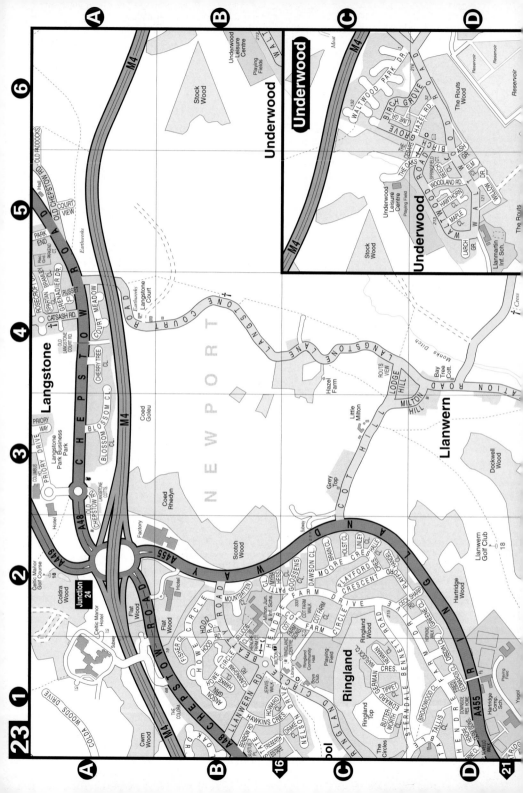

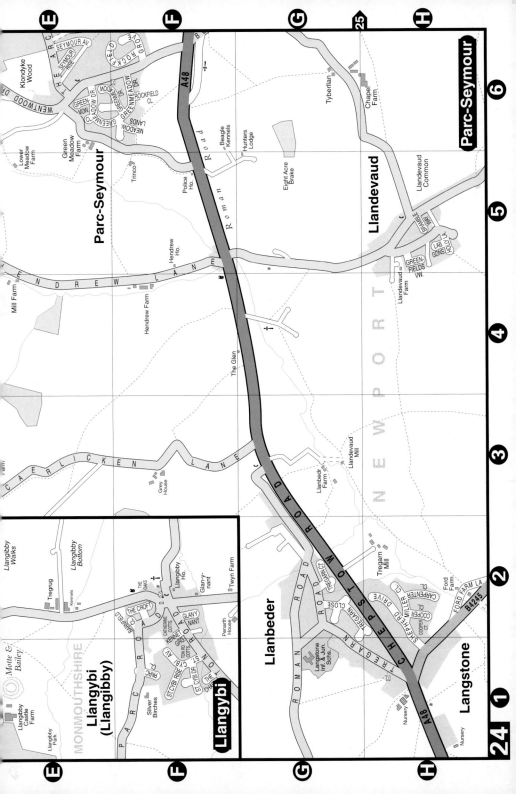

E   **F**   **G**   25   **H**

Parc-Seymour

6

5

4

3

2

1

24

SEYMOUR AV.
SEYMOUR RISE
THE ARCADIA
GROVE
ROCKFIELD GRO.
WENTWOOD DR.
Klondyke Wood
A48
Rockfield Road
GREENMEADOW DR.
GREENMEADOW DR.
MOOR
MEADOW
CLEADOW DR.
MEADOW
LANDS
ROCKFIELD CL.
Lower Meadow Farm
Green Meadow Farm
Trinco
Police Ho.
Beagle Kennels
Hunters Lodge
Tyberllan
Chapel Farm

Parc-Seymour

Roman Road

Eight Acre Brake

Llandevaud Common

HENDREW LANE
Mill Farm
Hendrew Ho.
Hendrew Farm
The Glen

Llandevaud

GRAMBLE WAY
LAB GDNS
HOLLY LA
GREEN-FIELDS
Llandevaud VW.
Llandevaud Farm

CAERLICKEN LANE
Grey House

N E W P O R T

Llanbedr Farm
Llandevaud Mill

Tregarn Mill
Ford Farm.
FORD FARM LA.
B4245

CHEPSTOW ROAD

ROMAN ROAD
TREGARN ROAD
TREGARN CLOSE
TREGARN ROAD
SHEPHERD MILLER DRIVE
COOPER CL.
BEDFORD CT.
CARPENTER CL.

Llanbeder

Langstone Inf & Jun. Schs.

Nursery
A48
Nursery

Langstone

Llangybi (Llangibby)

MONMOUTHSHIRE

Motte & Bailey
Llangibby Castle Farm
Llangibby Park
Llangibby Walks
Tregrug
Kennels
Llangibby Bottom
THE OAKS
Llangibby Ho.
Glan-y-nant
Twyn Farm
BARNFIELD
PARC ROAD
THE CROFT
CATHERINE COTTS.
KENNET GRO.
GLAN Y NANT
Penarth House
PARC ROAD
Silver Birches
ST. CYBI AV.
ST. CYBI RISE
TON RD. COTTS.
ST. CYBI DR.
THE LANE

Llangybi

E   **F**   **G**   **H**

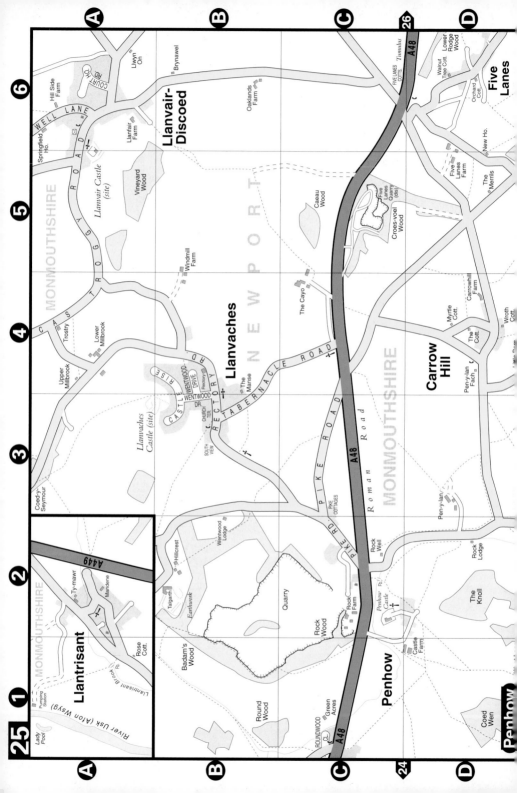

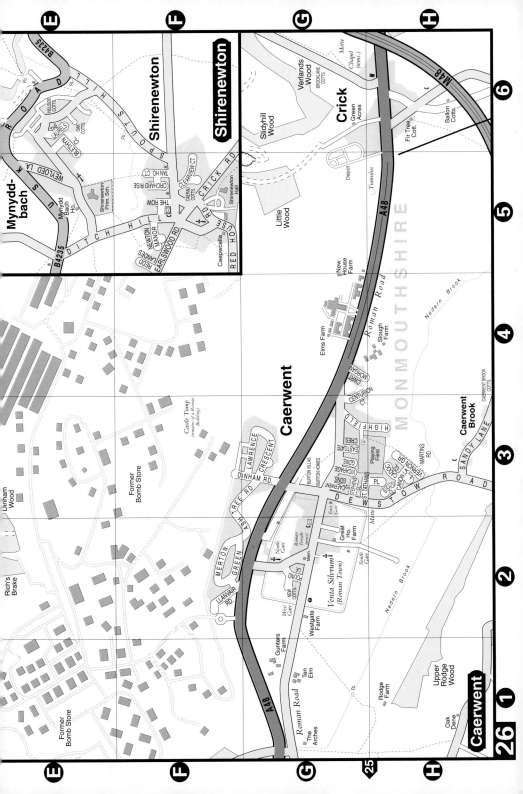

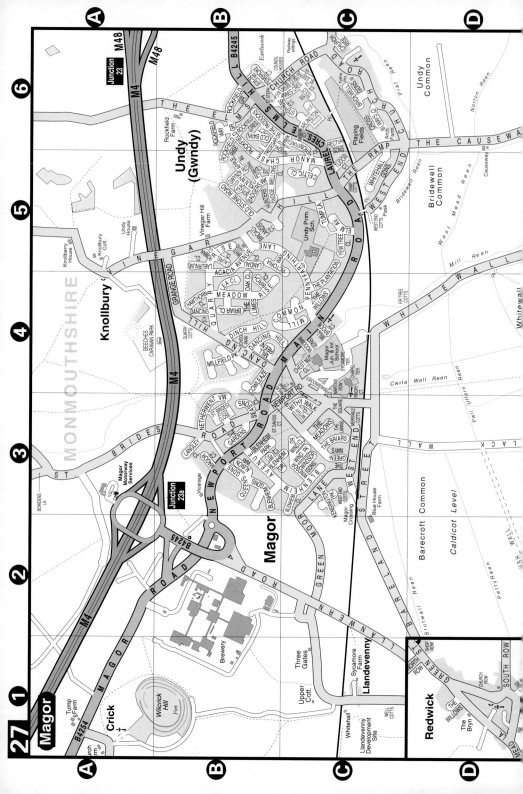

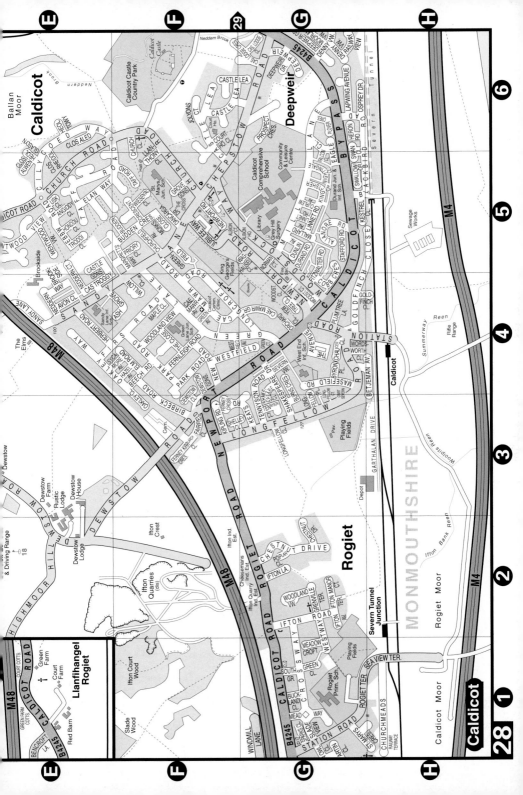

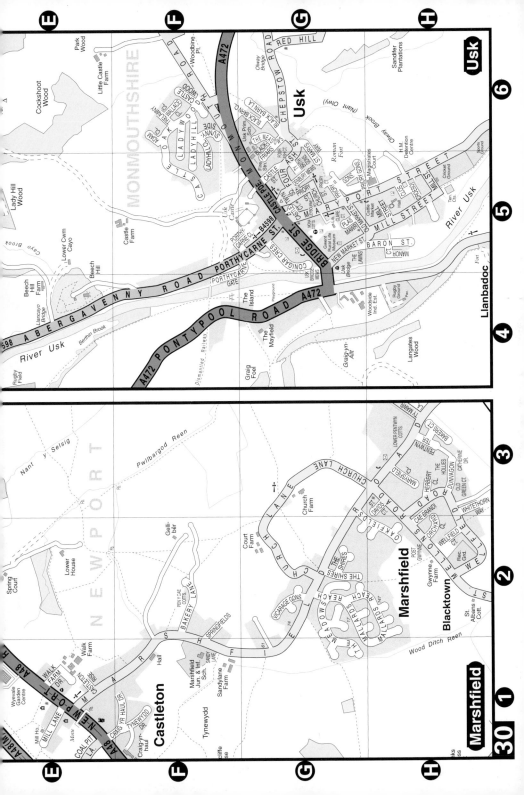

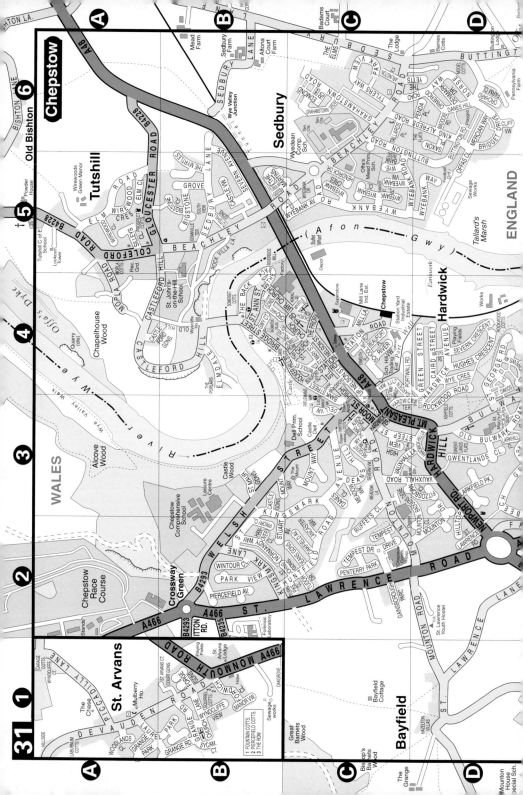

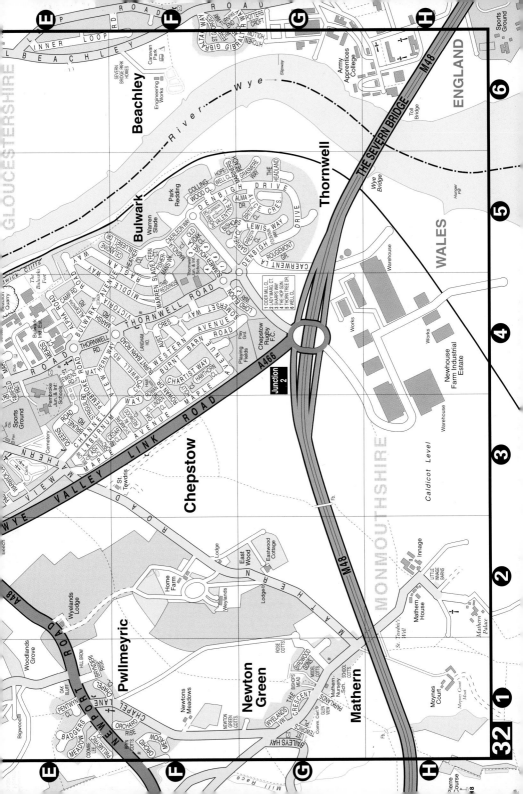

INDEX

Abbreviations used

App.	Approach	Dis.	Disused	Inf.	Infant	Pav.	Pavilion
Approach		Dr.	Drive	Junc.	Junction	Pl.	Place
Arc.	Arcade	E	East	La.	Lane	Prim.	Primary
Av.	Avenue	Ent.	Enterprise	Lib.	Library	Rec.	Recreation
Br.	Bridge	Est.	Estate	Lit.	Little	Rd.	Road
Bldgs.	Buildings	Fld(s).	Fields	Lwr.	Lower	Sch.	School
Bung(s).	Bungalows	Fb.	Footbridge	Mkt.	Market	S.	South
Bus.	Business	Gdns.	Gardens	Mdw(s).	Meadow(s)	Sq.	Square
Cara.	Caravan	Gt.	Great	Mem.	Memorial	Stn.	Station
Cem.	Cemetery	Grn.	Green	Mt.	Mount	St.	Street
Cl.	Close	Grd.	Ground	N.	North	Ten.	Tennis
Comm.	Community	Gr.	Grove	Off(s).	Office(s)	Ter.	Terrace
Comp.	Comprehensive	Hd.	Head	Orch.	Orchard	Up.	Upper
Cott(s).	Cottage(s)	Hosp.	Hospital	Par.	Parade	Vlls.	Villas
Cres.	Crescent	Ho.	House	Pk.	Park	Wk.	Walk
Ct.	Court	Ind.	Industrial	Pass.	Passage	W.	West

Use of this Index:

1. An alphabetical order is followed.
2. Each street name is followed by a map reference giving a page number and coordinates: Abbey Farm Lane 10 H4.
3. Names not appearing on the map are shown with an* and the reference of the nearest adjoining street: Blenheim Square*, Blenheim Rd. 8 E5.
4. Where a street name appears more than once the reference is given: Caernarvon Crescent 9 D3/10 E3.
5. There is insufficient space to name all streets in situ, these appear in numbered lists and the reference is given: Dene Court (24) 3D3.
6. House numbers along streets are shown: 250.

A

Abbey Cottages...............10 H4
Abbey Farm Lane...........10 H4
Abbey Green....................10 G2
Abbey Grove....................10 G2
Abbey Road (Cwmbran)....10 E1
Abbey Road (Newport)....16 H6
Abbots Mews...................19 B4
Abergavenny Road (Blaenavon)
....1 B4
Abergavenny Road (Penperlleni)
....5 A5
Abergavenny Road (Usk)..30 E4
Abergelli Cottages 4 F1
Aberthaw Avenue 21 A5
Aberthaw Circle 21 A4
Aberthaw Close 21 A5
Aberthaw Drive 21 A4
Aberthaw Road 21 A4/A6
Acacia Avenue (Newport) .21 A4
Acacia Avenue (Undy) 27 B5
Acacia Square 21 A4
Acorn Close 3 B2
Adam Close 30 F6
Adelaide Street 14 G5
Adeline Street.................19 D5
Adit Walk 12 E6
Adrian Boult Green........21 B5
Ael y Bryn 1 B5
Aerons House 8 F5
Afon Close 6 E4
Afon Court 3 B3
Afon Llwyd Terrace (18).....3 D3
Afon Llwyd Close 15 D4
Afon Mead.......................12 G1
Afon Terrace.....................9 C3
Agincourt Street 14 G5
Ailesbury Street..............14 G5
Alan Close (1)................17 A4
Alanbrooke Avenue 13 B3
Albany Street..................14 G5
Albert Avenue.................16 H1
Albert Court 2 H1
Albert Road 2 H1
Albert Street...................19 B6

Albert Terrace................19 A4
Albion Close 19 C5
Albion Court (Caldicot)...28 G5
Albion Court (Newport)...19 C6
Albion House..................28 G5
Albion Place.....................4 E3
Albion Road......................4 G4
Albion Square.................31 C3
Albion Way.....................27 B3
Alcock Close..................21 C3
Alder Close.......................4 D4
Alder Grove....................13 D4
Alderney Street 14 G5
Alders, The 10 F4
Alexandra Court*, Alexandra Rd.
....19 D6
Alexandra Road (Chepstow)
....32 E4
Alexandra Road (Newport)
....19 D6
Alexandra Road (Pontypool)
....6 G2
Alfred Street 14 H6
Alianore Road 28 G5
Alice Crescent................32 G5
Alice Street 19 D5
Allen Close 12 E6
Alleyn House (1)...............9 C4
Allgood Avenue 1 C3
Allt yr Yn Avenue 14 H3/19 A1
Allt yr Yn Close...............14 H3
Allt yr Yn Court...............14 G3
Allt yr Yn Crescent.........14 G3
Allt yr Yn Heights...........14 H3
Allt yr Yn Road 14 H3
Allt yr Yn View...............14 H2
Allt yr Yn Way................14 G3
Alma Close 19 C5
Alma Drive......................32 G5
Alma Place 6 G2
Alma Street (Blaenavon)....1 B4
Alma Street (Newport)....19 C5
Almond Court*, Larch Gr..13 C4
Almond Drive..................13 C3
Alpha Road......................32 E4

Alpine Cottages 4 F3
Alton Terrace 4 E5
Alway Close....................21 A5
Alway Crescent 21 A5
Alway Parade*, Aberthaw Av.
....21 A5
Alwyn Close 12 G4
Amberley Place 4 E4
Ambleside Lower...............2 H1
Ambleside Upper...............2 H2
Ambrose Way....................5 D4
Ambryn Road 5 D5
Amroth Walk.....................8 E6
Amy Johnson Close........21 C3
Anderson Close..............19 D3
Anderson Place..............13 C3
Aneurin Bevan Court (Newport)
....20 G1
Aneurin Bevan Court
(Pontypool)..................4 G5
Angidity Close 28 E5
Anglesey Court...............15 C2
Anne Street.......................1 B4
Annesley Road...............16 G1
Anson Green 23 B1
Anthony Drive.................15 C2
Anwyll Close...................15 C3
Apple Avenue 27 B5
Apprentice Close 32 F6
Aragon House*, Oakfield Road
....19 A3
Aragon Street..................14 G5
Aran Court 7 B5
Arcade, The (Cwmbran)....9 D2
Arcade, The (Parc-Seymour)
....24 E6
Arcadia Way 3 C5
Archer Road 7 D5
Archibald Street..............21 A1
Archway Court*, Moor St..31 C3
Argyle Street...................14 G5
Arlington Close (Newport).13 C3
Arlington Close (Undy)....27 C6
Arlington Court................31 C6
Armstrong Close.............21 B4

Arne Close......................23 D1
Arnold Close...................19 C2
Arthur Bliss Road 21 B5
Arthur Close 19 C5
Arthur Street (Caerleon)...15 D4
Arthur Street (Newport)...19 C5
Arthurs Court 29 B2
Artillery Place 14 H5
Arundel Close (1).............7 D4
Arundel Road 21 A2
Ash Close.......................32 E3
Ash Green 10 G2
Ash Grove (Caldicot) 28 F4
Ash Grove (Cwmbran).......9 C2
Ash Grove (Pontypool).....3 D6
Ash Grove (Underwood)..23 D6
Ash Tree Road................26 G2
Ashdown Court*,
Commercial Road 19 C6
Ashfield Cottages...........31 D3
Ashfield House*, Mt. Pleasant
....31 D3
Ashfield Houses*, Cross St.1 C4
Ashford Close...................9 C4
Ashford Close North..........9 C4
Ashford Close South..........9 C4
Ashgrove Close................6 F1
Ashleigh Court..................8 F3
Ashley Road 21 A3
Ashorn House....................8 E6
Ashwell 16 F5
Ashwell Villas.................16 F5
Aspen Way.....................13 C4
Asquith Street...................6 E2
Aston Crescent...............14 F4
Ashgrove Hames Close....19 C3
Auckland Road................17 C6
Augustan Close...............15 D2
Augustan Drive...............15 D2
Augustan Way................15 D2
Augustus John Close......16 F3
Augustus Place...............23 B1
At Crescent.....................32 F4
Austin Friars...................19 A5
Austin Road......................6 G2

Avalon Court.....................4 F4
Avalon Drive....................16 G2
Avenue, The (Caldicot)....28 G4
Avenue, The (Coedkernew)
....18 F5
Avenue, The (Garndiffaith)..2 G1
Avenue, The (New Inn) 5 C3
Avenue, The (Sebastopol)
....6 F1/G1
Avenue, The*, Bushy Park..4 F4
Avenue, The*, Clytha Square
....19 B5
Avon Close (Caldicot).......28 E4
Avon Close (Newport) 14 E1
Avon Place 10 E3
Avon Road........................1 C4
Avondale 1 C4
Avondale Close 9 A2
Avondale Crescent...........9 A2
Avondale Road ...6 G3/H3/9 A1
Avondale Way...................9 A2

B

Back, The 31 B4
Backhall Street 15 D4
Bacon Place 13 C3
Badgers Dene 31 D3
Badgers Meadow (Chepstow)
....32 E1
Badgers Meadow (Ponthir)
....15 A5
Badgers Mede..................7 D5
Badgers Walk 27 B5
Badgers Wood Close......17 D2
Badminton Road.............16 F2
Badminton Villas.............31 B4
Bagley Court.....................7 B4
Bailey Crescent................2 G2
Bailey Street (Garndiffaith)..2 G1
Bailey Street (Newport)....19 A4
Baileys Hay....................32 G1
Baileys Houses (1)...........3 D3
Baileys Terrace (2)...........3 D3
Baird Close.....................13 C2
Baker Street House (9)....1 D4
Bakers Court 30 H3

Bakery Houses (Garndiffaith) 2 G1
Bakery Houses*, New Rd...3 A3
Bakery Lane......30 F2
Bala Drive......12 G4
Bala House......8 E5
Balance Meadow......2 F1
Balance Road......2 F1
Baldwin Close 19 D5
Baldwin Street 19 C5
Balfe Road......21 A6
Balmond Terrace......4 E4
Balmoral Lane......21 A3
Balmoral Road......21 A3
Baltic Terrace 10 H1
Bamber House (2)......9 C4
Baneswell Courtyard......19 A5
Baneswell Road......19 A4
Bank Lane......16 F1
Bank Square......31 C4
Bank Street (Chepstow)...31 C3
Bank Street (Newport)......16 F1
Bankers Row 1 A3
Bantock Close 21 A6
Banwell Court 7 B4
Barbirolli Green......21 B5
Bardsey Close......16 G2
Bareland Street 27 C2
Barn Close......3 C4
Barn Owl Road......28 G1
Barnard Street 14 H6
Barnets 7 D4
Barnfield (Blaenavon)......1 C3
Barnfield (Ponthir) 15 A2/B6
Barnfield Close 24 F2
Barnfield Place 7 B6
Barnfield Terrace 1 C3
Baron Street 30 H5
Barons Court 27 C5
Barrack Hill 14 G3
Barrie Gardens 19 D1
Barry Walk 12 G4
Barthropp Street 21 B3
Bassaleg Road......17 C6/19 C1
Batchelor Road......21 A2
Batchelors Row 2 H2
Bath Green 10 E4
Bath Street 14 H6
Bay Tree Close 15 D1
Beachley Road (Beachley)32 E6
Beachley Road (Sedbury)
......31 B5/C5
Beacons Close......12 G4
Beatty Road......23 B1
Beaufort Close......8 F5
Beaufort Place (Chepstow)
......31 C4
Beaufort Place (Newport)..16 F2
Beaufort Road......16 F2
Beaufort Square......31 C4
Beaufort Terrace 19 A4
Beaumaris Close......17 B2
Beaumaris Drive......10 E4
Beaumaris House......10 E4
Beddick......7 D4
Bedford Close (2)......7 D4
Bedford Road 19 A6
Beech Close (Cwmbran) ...7 B6
Beech Close (Underwood)23 D5
Beech Grove (Chepstow)..31 D3
Beech Grove (Newport)......20 F2
Beech Road (Caldicot) 28 F4
Beech Road (Pontypool)......6 G1
Beech Tree Terrace 3 D3
Beecham Street......21 A6

Beechcroft Road 16 H3
Beechdale Road......16 H3
Beeches Caravan Park 27 A4
Beeches Road......3 C4
Beeches, The (Cwmbran).10 E1
Beeches, The (Pontypool) ..3 C3
Beechfield Avenue 16 H3
Beechleigh Close 7 D3
Beechwood Crescent......21 H3
Beechwood Road...16 H3/21 A3
Beechwood Walk 3 C4
Belgrave Court (21)......3 D3
Bell Lane......3 B2
Belle Vue Close (Cwmbran)
......10 E1
Belle Vue Close (Pontypool)
......3 C4
Belle Vue Cottages......7 B4
Belle Vue Court (11)......3 D3
Belle Vue Lane......19 B4
Belle Vue Road......10 F1
Belle Vue Terrace (Cwmbran)
......8 F2
Belle Vue Terrace (Newport)
......19 C5
Bellin Close 15 C3
Belmont Hill......16 F5
Belmont House......16 F6
Belvedere Terrace 14 G4
Ben Jonson Way......19 C1
Benbow Road......23 B1
Bencroft Lane......28 E1
Benson Avenue (2) 17 A4
Bentley Close......12 G3
Beresford Road 19 A6
Berkeley Court......7 C4
Berkley Close 17 B3
Berkley Crescent......6 G2
Berkley Road 17 B3
Berthin 7 D5
Berthon Road......6 H5
Bessemer Close......13 C2
Bethel Court (1)......2 G1
Bethel Lane 7 A4
Bethesda Close......12 H3
Bethesda Place 12 H3
Betjeman Avenue 28 H4
Bettws Centre......13 D1
Bettws Close......14 E2
Bettws Hill 12 E6/14 E1
Bettws Lane......14 E2
Betwyns (1)......8 F5
Bevans Lane 6 H2
Bideford Close......19 D3
Bideford Road 19 D3
Bighams Row 4 H5
Bigstone Close 31 B5
Bigstone Grove 31 B5
Bilston Street 21 B2
Birbeck Road 28 F3
Birch Close 27 B4
Birch Grove (Cwmbran) 8 G3
Birch Grove (Rogerstone).12 H2
Birch Grove (Underwood)
......23 C6/D6
Birch Hill 13 D4
Birch Trees 17 C4
Birches, The 7 C5
Birchgrove Close 13 D4
Birchwood Houses*,
Freeholdland Road ...3 C3
Birdwood Gardens 32 G1
Bishop Close (Caernon)..26 H3
Bishop Street......14 H6
Bishops Close (Chepstow)32 F5

Bishops Mead 32 G1
Bishpool Estate 16 H6
Bishpool Lane 16 H6
Bishton Lane 31 A6
Bishton Street 21 A1
Black Ash Path 16 F5
Black Barn Close 30 G6
Black Barn Lane......30 G6
Black Friars 30 G5
Black Horse Lane*,
Somerton Road......21 B3
Black Lane 1 B4
Black Path 2 H2
Black Rock Road......29 B4
Black Wall......27 C4
Blackbird Road......28 G5
Blackbirds Close (Newport)
......13 B3
Blackbirds Close (Rogerstone)
......17 B5
Blackett Avenue 13 D3
Blacksmiths Way......18 G4
Blackthorn Grove 15 D1
Blackwater Close 11 D6
Blaen y Cwm View......8 F2
Blaen y Pant Avenue 14 F3
Blaen y Pant Crescent......14 F3
Blaen y Pant House......14 F3
Blaen y Pant Place 14 F3
Blaendare Farm Road......4 H4
Blaendare Road 4 H4
Blaenwern......9 B2
Blake Road 21 B4
Blanch Close 20 G2
Blenheim Avenue 27 C3
Blenheim Close 27 C3
Blenheim Court (Cwmbran).8 E5
Blenheim Court (Magor)...27 B3
Blenheim Drive 27 B3
Blenheim Gardens......27 B3
Blenheim Park 27 B3
Blenheim Road (Cwmbran).8 E5
Blenheim Road (Newport).21 A3
Blenheim Square*,
Blenheim Road......8 E5
Bleriot Close 21 C3
Blethyn Close 26 E6
Blewitt Street 19 A4
Blodwen Road......5 D4
Blodwen Way......5 D4
Bloomfield Close 16 H6
Blorange Terrace......1 A4
Blossom Close 23 A3
Blue Boar 3 A1
Bluebell Court 8 E2
Bluebell Drive......32 F5
Bluetts Houses*, Viaduct Road
......2 H2
Bluetts Lane*, Bluetts Rd...2 H1
Bluetts Road......2 H1
Boddington Terrace (1) 15 D4
Bolt Close 19 C6
Bolt Street......19 C6
Bolton Road......19 B3
Bolton Street 14 G4
Bolts Row*, Chepstow Rd.21 A4
Bond Street 14 H5
Boot Lane*, Broad Street...1 C4
Booths Lane 3 D1
Boswell Close......19 C2
Bosworth Drive......14 G4
Bowdens Lane ...24 F6/27 A3
Bowen Close......1 B4
Bowen Place*, Francis Dr. 19 C5
Bowleaze......7 D5

Box Tree Close 15 D1
Boyle Close 13 D2
Brades, The......15 C4
Brain Close......23 C2
Bramble Way......24 H5
Bramley Close......23 A4
Brangwyn Avenue......10 G3
Brangwyn Crescent......16 G2
Brankleys Houses 1 C6
Brassknocker Street......27 C4
Brechfa Close......15 A5
Brecon Court 15 C2
Brecon Road 16 G2
Brecon Walk......9 D2
Briar Close......27 B4
Briars, The......27 C3
Brick Houses*, Avon Rd.....1 C4
Brick Yard Lane......17 A6
Brickyard Cottages 7 A4
Bridewell Gardens 27 C6
Bridge Buildings*, Godfrey Rd.
......19 A4
Bridge Street (Blaenavon) ..1 C4
Bridge Street (Chepstow)..31 B4
Bridge Street (Newport) 19 A4
Bridge Street (Pontypool)....6 E2
Bridge Street (Usk) 30 G5
Bridge Terrace 17 C5
Bridget Drive......31 D6
Briers Gate 8 G2
Brightstown 2 G1
Bristol House*, Hanbury Road
......4 E2
Bristol Street 14 H6
Bristol View Close 7 D3
British School Close 3 A1
Briton Close (Chepstow)...32 G5
Britten Close (Newport)......21 B5
Broad Quay Road......22 E1
Broad Street (Abersychan)..3 B3
Broad Street (Blaenavon) ...1 C4
Broad Street (Newport) 19 C6
Broad Street (Pontypool) 6 E2
Broad View......7 B5
Broadcommon Close 21 C5
Broadlands Court 27 B5
Broadmead Park 21 B5
Broadstreet Common 22 F5
Broadwalk......15 D4
Broadwater Road 21 D5
Broadway (Caerleon) 16 E4
Broadway (Pontypool) 4 F5
Broadweir Road......10 E1
Broadwell Court......15 D4
Broadwood Close......23 D1
Bron y Garth*, The Highway
......9 C4
Bronllys Place......2 H2
Bronte Grove 19 D1
Browning Close 19 C2
Brunel Avenue......12 H4
Brunel Road (Chepstow)...32 E3

Brunel Road (Cwmbran) 8 E4
Brunel Street 19 D6
Brunswick Court (14)......3 D3
Brutes Row 1 C3
Bryn Bevan 14 F4
Bryn Carreg......2 H2
Bryn Cottages......32 F1
Bryn Eglwys......9 C3
Bryn Garw 9 C3
Bryn Gomer 9 A3
Bryn Gwyn Place......4 F4
Bryn Gwyn Road......4 G4
Bryn Milwr 8 G6
Bryn Onnen Court......8 G3
Bryn Rhedyn 10 G5
Bryn Terrace (3) (Pontypool)
......3 D3
Bryn Terrace (Blaenavon)...1 B4
Bryn Terrace (Garndiffaith).2 G1
Bryn Welon Close 1 C5
Bryn, The......13 D1
Brynavon 1 C4
Bryncelyn Place......7 B6
Bryncelyn Road......7 B6
Brynderi Rise......32 E1
Brynderwen Cottages 3 A3
Brynderwen Court 16 H1
Brynderwen Grove 16 H1
Brynderwen Road 16 H1
Brynglas 8 G5
Brynglas & Malpas Relief Road
......13 B3
Brynglas Avenue 14 F4
Brynglas Close 14 E4
Brynglas Court......14 E4
Brynglas Crescent 14 F4
Brynglas Drive......14 E4
Brynglas Gardens*,
Brynglas Road......14 G4
Brynglas Road......14 G4
Bryngwyn Road......19 B3
Brynhedydd......17 C2
Brynheulog......4 H6/5 D1
Brynhyfryd......9 B4
Brynhyfryd Avenue 19 B4
Brynhyfryd Close......6 H5
Brynhyfryd Road......19 B4
Brynhyfryd Terrace
(Abersychan)......3 C2
Brynteg 3 B2
Brynteg Place......6 G6
Brynwern......4 F4
Buchan Close 19 C2
Buckingham Crescent ...16 H2
Buckingham Place 16 H2
Buckland Close 28 G1
Budden Crescent......28 F5
Buller Street......4 E2
Bulmore Road......16 F5
Bulwark Avenue 32 E4
Bulwark Road......31 D3
Bungalows, The......1 A3
Burford Street 1 B4
Burleigh Road......19 A3
Burnfold Road......19 C2
Burns Close 19 D1
Burns Crescent 28 G3
Burns Lane 8 E6
Burnt Barn Road......32 F4
Burton Homes (Caernont)26 G3
Burton Homes (Newport)..19 B4
Burton Road......16 F2
Burton Villas 26 G3
Bush Lane 4 G4
Bushy Park 4 F4

Butlers Court (2).................2 G1
Butlers Lane (3)..................2 G1
Butlers Row 3 B2
Buttercup Court.....................8 F2
Buttermere Way 16 F2
Butterworth Close.................23 C1
Buttington Cottages............31 D6
Buttington Hill......................31 D6
Buttington Road 31 D5
Buttington Terrace...............31 D6
Buxton Close 19 D3
Byrde Close 21 A5
Byron Place (Caldicot)......28 G4
Byron Place (Cwmbran).......8 E6
Byron Road 19 C2
Bythway Road 3 C5
Byways................7 D4/8 E4
C
C Row..................................1 C2
Caban Close 12 G4
Cadoc Close......................26 H3
Cadoc Road..........................7 B5
Cae Brandi 30 H2
Cae Brynton Road.............19 C3
Cae Derwen 10 F1
Cae Mawr Avenue 28 F4
Cae Mawr Grove 28 G4
Cae Mawr Road.................28 F4
Cae Melin 6 G6
Cae Perllan Road...............19 C3
Cae Rhedyn..........................9 C4
Cae White 1 B3
Cae yr Ebol..........................9 C1
Caepalish 3 D3
Caepalish Place (9)..............3 D3
Caerau Cottages 26 F5
Caerau Crescent 19 B3
Caerau Road 19 B3
Caerleon House (Newport)18 F5
Caerleon Houses*, High Street
...................................15 D4
Caerleon Road (Llanfrechfa)
....10 E4
Caerleon Road (Newport)
...........................14 H6/16 F2
Caerleon Road (Ponthir)
...........................15 A2/A5
Caerleon Way 32 F5
Caerlicken Lane 24 E3
Caernarvon Close 9 D4
Caernarvon Crescent
.........................9 D3/10 E3
Caernarvon Drive 17 B2
Caerphilly Close 17 C2
Caerphilly Road 17 B1/C5
Caerwent Brook Cottages.26 H4
Caerwent Gardens............26 G3
Caerwent House.................18 F5
Caerwent Lane 32 G5
Caerwent Road (Cwmbran) 9 A3
Caerwent Road (Pontypool)3 D6
Caesar Crescent 15 C2
Caird Street 31 D4
Calcot House (3)..................9 C4
Caldicot Bypass 28 G4
Caldicot Road (Caldicot)
...........................28 E1/E5
Caldicot Road (Portskewett)
....29 B1
Caldicot Road (Rogiet)....28 G1
Caldicot Street 21 B2
Caldicot Way 9 B2
Caldy Close 16 G2
Cam Court 7 B4
Cambria Close 15 D5

Cambria Street........................6 F2
Cambrian Centre*, Queensway
....19 A4
Cambrian Road 19 A5
Cambridge Court...............15 C1
Cambridge Road 19 A6
Camelot Close 15 D5
Camelot Court 15 D5
Camelot Place 14 H6
Camp Road (Chepstow)...32 E4
Camp Road (Sudbrook)....29 D4
Campbell Street 4 E4
Camperdown Road 21 B3
Campion Close (Cwmbran) 8 G3
Campion Close (Newport).14 H4
Camrose Walk......................8 E6
Canal Bank (Newport).......13 C2
Canal Bank*, Blaen y Pant Cres.
....14 F3
Canal Bank*, Osborne Rd....4 E5
Canal Close 6 F2
Canal Parade 19 A6/B6
Canal Side 10 E1
Canal Street 14 G4
Canal Terrace 19 B6
Canberra Close 8 E6
Canberra Crescent 19 B1
Candwr Lane 15 A2/A6
Candwr Park 15 A6
Candwr Road 15 A2/B6
Canford Close 3 C4
Canon Lane 26 H3
Canon Street 14 H6
Canterbury Close (1).........14 H5
Canterbury Way 29 C3
Cantref Close 12 G4
Capel Close 19 C6
Capel Court (23)....................3 D3
Capel Crescent 19 C5
Capel Ed Lane 5 A5
Capel Newydd Avenue 1 C5
Capel Newydd Road 1 C4
Capel Street (Newport) 19 C5
Capel Street (Pontypool) 4 G5
Caradoc Close 9 C1
Caradoc Road 3 B2
Caradoc Walk.......................1 B4
Caradog Close 15 C3
Cardiff Road
........18 E6/19 D2/C5/20 E1
Cardigan Close 9 B3
Cardigan Court 15 C2
Cardigan Crescent 9 A3
Cardigan Place 16 G2
Carey Road 21 A3
Carfax Path (2) 8 F5
Carisbrooke Road 21 A2
Carlisle Street 19 D6
Carlton Court (15)................3 D3
Carlton Road.......................16 G1
Carlton Terrace 16 E4
Caroline Road 5 D4
Caroline Street 19 B6
Caroline Way........................5 D4
Carpenter Close 24 H2
Carpenters Arms Lane*,
High Street 19 A5
Cartwright Green 13 D3
Cas Troggy 28 E4
Cas Troggy Road 25 A4
Castell y Bwch Cottages ...11 A4
Castle Close 17 B5
Castle Cottages 16 E4
Castle Court (Cwmbran).....8 G3
Castle Court (Newport)......17 B5

Castle Court (Portskewett) 29 B2
Castle Court (Usk)..............30 G5
Castle Court*, Welsh St. ...31 B2
Castle Gardens (Caldicot).28 E5
Castle Gardens (Chepstow)
....31 B3
Castle Lane 16 E5
Castle Lea..........................28 F6
Castle Lodge Close...........28 G6
Castle Lodge Crescent 28 G6
Castle Mews (Caerleon).....16 E5
Castle Mews*, George St....4 F5
Castle Oak 30 F5
Castle Parade 30 G5
Castle Park Close 19 C1
Castle Park Road...............19 C1
Castle Rise 25 B3
Castle Street (Blaenavon)...1 B4
Castle Street (Caerleon)....16 E5
Castle Street (Newport) 19 C6
Castle Street (Usk)............30 G5
Castle View........................31 B5
Castle Way 29 C1
Castle Wood (Usk)............30 F6
Castleford Gardens 31 A4
Castleford Hill 31 A4
Castleton Rise 30 E1
Castlewood (Talywain).......2 H1
Caswell Way.......................21 D3
Catalpa Close 13 C4
Cathedral Court 19 B4
Catherine Close 20 G2
Catherine Cottages 24 F2
Catherine Drive 30 H3
Catref Melus 21 B3
Catsash Road (Langstone)
....23 A4
Catsash Road (Newport) ...16 G6
Causeway Cottages...........27 D6
Causeway, The 27 D6
Caxton Place 19 A5
Cecil Lane 17 A4
Cecil Sharpe Road............23 C2
Cedarwood Drive 12 G1
Cedar Close 32 F3
Cedar Road 19 A6
Cedar Walk...........................7 B5
Cedars, The........................23 C6
Cefn Close (Cwmbran)........9 B4
Cefn Close (Newport).......12 H5
Cefn Court (Newport).......19 B3
Cefn Court (Rogerstone)...12 H5
Cefn Drive 12 H4
Cefn Milwr 8 G6
Cefn Rise 12 H3
Cefn Road 12 G3/H4
Cefn Walk...........................12 H5
Cefn Wood 17 A4
Celandine Court (Chepstow)
....32 F5
Celandine Court (Cwmbran)8 E2
Celtic Close 27 C5
Celtic Way 18 G5/H6
Celyn Court..........................7 B5
Celynen Grove 20 E2
Cemetery Lane 19 B5
Cenfedd Street 14 G6
Central Avenue 21 C5
Central Drive 3 C4
Central Way 32 F5
Centurion Court 26 G4
Centurion Gate 15 D5
Ceredig Court (1).................10 E4
Chadwick Close 13 D3
Chaffinch Way 20 F2

Channel View (Chepstow).32 E3
Channel View (Cwmbran)....7 B5
Channel View (Newport) ...17 C3
Channel View (Pontypool)
............................4 E6/5 A1
Chapel Close (Chepstow).32 E1
Chapel Close (Garndiffaith) 2 G1
Chapel Lane (Chepstow)...32 F1
Chapel Lane (Cwmbran).....9 A3
Chapel Mead.........................5 A5
Chapel Road...........................4 E2
Chapel Row...........................1 B2
Chapel Street 9 C1
Chapel Terrace (Magor)....27 C4
Chapel Terrace (Newport).17 B1
Chapel Terrace*, Hanbury Rd.
....4 E2
Chapman Close 13 C3
Chapman Court*, Penllyn Av.
Charles Street (Blaenavon).1 C4
Charles Street (Cwmbran) ..9 B1
Charles Street (Newport) ..19 A5
Charles Street (Pontypool)..6 G2
Charles Street (Rogerstone)
....17 B3
Charlotte Green 19 C5
Charlotte Street 19 C5
Charlotte Walk...................19 C5
Charnwood House................8 E5
Charnwood Road...............14 F6
Charston 17 D5
Chartist Drive 12 H4/17 A4
Chartist Way 32 F4
Chase, The 24 F1
Chaucer Close 28 G4
Chaucer Court*, Chaucer Road
....16 H2
Chaucer Road 16 H2
Chelmer Close 12 E6
Chelmer Walk 12 E6
Chelston Place 14 G4
Chepstow Close 9 A3
Chepstow Rise 9 A3
Chepstow Road (Caldicot) 28 F5
Chepstow Road (Langstone)
..............................23 A3/24 G2
Chepstow Road (Newport)
............14 H6/21 A2/23 B1
Chepstow Road (Usk).......30 G6
Cheriton Path........................8 E5
Cherry Tree Close (Caerleon)
....15 D4
Cherry Tree Close (Cwmbran)
....9 C4
Cherry Tree Close (Langstone)
....23 A4
Cherry Tree Close (Newport)
....13 D4
Cherwell Walk 11 D6
Chester Close 5 C5
Chester Holme 19 B3
Chestnut Close (Magor)....27 C4
Chestnut Close (Pontypool) 5 C5
Chestnut Drive 28 G2
Chestnut Green 7 B5
Chestnut Grove 15 D1
Chichester Close 16 E2
Chiltern Close (Newport)...16 H5
Chiltern Close (Risca)......12 E1
Christchurch Hill 16 G6
Christchurch Road......16 H1/H3
Christina Crescent 17 B5
Church Avenue 3 C5
Church Close (Caldicot) ...28 F6

Church Close (Cwmbran) 9 C3
Church Close (Newport)....17 A5
Church Close (Pontypool) ...6 F4
Church Cottages 16 E5
Church Crescent (Bassaleg)
....17 C3
Church Crescent (Duffryn) 18 E4
Church Farm Close 14 E1
Church Lane (Newport)....18 H4
Church Lane (Marshfield).30 G2
Church Lane (New Inn) 6 E5
Church Lane (Pontypool) 3 D4
Church Lane (St. Arvans)..31 A1
Church Mews*, Lower Park Ter.
....4 G5
Church Rise........................27 C6
Church Road (Abersychan).3 A1
Church Road (Blaenavon)...1 B3
Church Road (Caldicot)28 E5/F5
Church Road (Chepstow) .31 C4
Church Road (Cwmbran)....7 B6
Church Road (Henllys).........8 E2
Church Road (Llanfrechfa)10 G6
Church Road (Newport) ...14 H6
Church Road (Talywain) 3 A1
Church Road (Undy) 27 C6
Church Row (Chepstow)...31 C4
Church Row (Redwick) 27 D1
Church Row (Sudbrook) ...29 D4
Church Row*, Church Rd....3 A1
Church Street (Caerleon)..15 D4
Church Street (Newport) ..19 C6
Church Street (Rogerstone)
....12 H2
Church Street (Usk)...........30 G5
Church Terrace (4) (Pontypool)
....3 D3
Church Terrace (Llanvaches)
....25 B3
Church View.......................17 C5
Church View*, Church Rd...1 B3
Churchfield Avenue 28 F5
Churchmead (Newport)....17 C5
Churchmeads (Caldicot) ..28 H1
Churchward Drive..............21 B4
Churchwood.........................4 E5
Churchwood Close 4 E5
Churchwood Road 7 C6
Cider Mill Close (1) 32 F5
Cilgerran Court (2).............10 E4
Circle, The 8 F6
Clapham Terrace 1 C2
Clare Court.........................30 G5
Claremont...........................13 C4
Clarence Court*, Caerleon Rd.
....14 H6
Clarence Place (Newport).14 H5
Clarence Place (Pontypool)
............................4 G6/5 C1
Clarence Road 4 G5
Clarence Street (Newport) 19 C6
Clarence Street (Pontypool) 4 F5
Clarendon Close 32 F5
Clarendon Court 19 B3
Clarewain............................6 E4
Clarewain Terrace 6 E4
Clark Avenue 9 A1
Clayton Street....................14 H6
Clearview 26 F5
Clearwater Road 22 E6
Clearwell Court...................17 C2
Cleaves Terrace 3 B2
Clement Atlee Drive 16 G6
Cleppa Park 18 F5
Clevedon Close 16 H2

Clevedon Road 16 H2
Clewer Court.....................19 B3
Clewer Court Mews.........19 A3
Cliff View 31 D6
Clifton Place 19 B4
Clifton Road......................19 B4
Clifton Square.....................6 E2
Clifton Street....................12 F1
Clifton Terrace 1 B4
Clipper Close...................16 E2
Clist Road.........................11 D5
Clist Walk.........................11 D6
Clomendy Road........9 D1/10 E1
Clos Aled.........................28 E6
Clos Alwen.......................28 E5
Clos Croeso.....................30 H5
Clos Rheidol.....................28 E5
Close, The (Caldicot)........28 F4
Close, The (Cwmbran).......10 E1
Close, The (Portskewett) ..29 C2
Clover Court.......................8 F2
Club Road...........................4 F3
Club Row (Abersychan) 3 C3
Club Row (Talywain)..........2 H2
Clydach Close............14 E1/E2
Clyffard Crescent............19 B4
Clyffes................................7 D4
Clytha Crescent...............19 B5
Clytha Park Road 19 A3
Clytha Square..................19 B5
Co-op Buildings 2 H1
Co-op Terrace 2 H1
Co-operative Flats.............2 G1
Coal Pit Lane...................30 E1
Cobb Crescent................28 G4
Cobner Close.....................3 D5
Coch y North Lane 17 D1
Coch y North Road 4 G1
Cocker Avenue..................8 F6
Coed Cae 7 B6
Coed Cae Place 4 G5
Coed Cae Road...................1 B4
Coed Camlas 5 C2
Coed Eithin Street 1 C4
Coed Eva Mill.....................8 G5
Coed Garw 9 B3
Coed Glas...............8 F6/10 F1
Coed Lee 8 F5
Coed Lee Court*, Coed Lee 8 F5
Coed Llwyd Close 1 B5
Coed Road 1 C4
Coed Terrace (Blaenavon)..1 C5
Coed Terrace (Talywain)....3 A2
Coed y Canddo Road 5 C3
Coed y Gric.........................6 E2
Coed yr Eos.......................3 A3
Coedygraig Houses*,
    Station Road..................6 E2
Coity Terrace.....................1 C2
Cold Bath Road...............15 D4
Cold Store, The 10 F3
Coldra Road 19 C3
Coldra Woods Drive
    ....16 F6/23 A1
Coldra, The......................23 B1
Coldstream Close..............9 B3
Coleford Path 7 D5
Coleford Road 31 A2
Coleridge Green 8 E6
Coleridge Road 21 A3
College Crescent.............15 D4
College Glade...................15 B3
College Road (Caerleon) ..15 C3
College Road (Pontypool)
    ....4 E6/5 A1

College Terrace (6) 3 D3
Collier Street.....................14 H6
Collingwood Avenue 21 B3
Collingwood Close (Chepstow)
    ....32 F5
Collingwood Close (Newport)
    ....21 B3
Collingwood Crescent 21 B3
Collingwood Road............21 B3
Collins Close 19 D1
Colne Street.....................19 A6
Colston Avenue...............21 C2
Colston Court....................21 B3
Colston Place 21 B3
Colts Foot Close..............14 H4
Columbus House...........23 A3
Comfrey Close 14 H3
Commercial Close.............2 H1
Commercial Place 9 B1
Commercial Road (Newport)
    ....19 B5
Commercial Road (Talywain)
    ....2 H1/3 A1
Commercial Street
    (Pontnewydd) 9 B1
Commercial Street
    (Griffithstown) 6 E2
Commercial Street (5)
    (Blaenavon)...............1 C4
Commercial Street (Cwmbran)
    ....10 E1
Commercial Street (Newport)
    ....19 A5
Commercial Street (Pontypool)
    ....4 F5
Commercial Wharf 21 C1
Compton Close 12 H4
Conifer Close...................15 D1
Coniston Close 16 F1
Coniston House*, Blenheim Rd.
    ....8 E5
Conrad House*, Beaufort Sq.
    ....31 C4
Constable Drive 16 F2
Constables Lane 19 C6
Constance Street.............14 G6
Conway Close 9 C1
Conway Court...................21 A3
Conway Croft...................21 A3
Conway Road (Newport) ...21 A2
Conway Road (Pontypool) ..4 F4
Conway Sac 21 A3
Conway Terrace 9 C3
Coolgreany Close............14 E3
Coolgreany Crescent 14 E3
Coomassie Street............19 D6
Coombe Lea.....................32 E1
Cooper Close 24 H2
Coopers Houses 3 C2
Copper Beech Close 15 D1
Coppins, The....................13 D4
Corelli Street.....................14 H6
Coriander Close 14 H3
Cork Road.........................20 E6
Cormorant Way................20 G2
Corn Street......................19 A5
Cornbrook Road...............13 D1
Cornwall Road..................16 G1
Coronation Terrace
    (Abersychan)..............3 B3
Coronation Terrace (4)
    (Pontypool)................3 D3
Coronation Terrace (Talywain)
    ....3 A2

Corporation Road
    ..14 H6/19 A6/21 A1/22 E2
Corris House.....................9 A2
Cory Park 10 H4
Cot Farm Circle 23 C2
Cot Farm Close 23 C2
Cot Farm Gardens 23 C2
Cot Farm Walk 23 C2
Cot Hill 23 C3
Cotman Close 16 G3
Cotswold Close 16 H5
Cotswold Way (Newport) ..16 H5
Cotswold Way (Risca)......12 E1
Coulson Close 19 C5
Council Houses (Undy) 27 B6
Council Houses*, Manor Road
    ....3 A1
Council Houses*, Wesley St.
    ....10 E1
Court Cottages 28 E1
Court Crescent 17 C4
Court Farm Close.............10 G3
Court Farm Road 10 G3
Court Gardens (Rogerstone)
    ....12 H2
Court Gardens (St. Arvans)
    ....31 B1
Court House Close 28 F6
Court House Road............25 A6
Court Meadow 23 A4
Court Rise (4) 1 B4
Court Road 10 F2/F3
Court View 23 A5
Courtfields Close 12 H2
Courtlands, The 8 E4
Courtney Street 14 H6
Courtyard, The 18 G6
Courtybella Cottages*,
    Courtybella Gdns. 19 C6
Courtybella Gardens........19 C6
Courtybella Terrace..........19 C5
Coverack Road.................21 B1
Covert Walk (3)..................8 F4
Cowleaze 27 B4
Cowper Close...................19 D1
Cowshed Lane 17 C3
Craig Ceiliog Lane
    ....8 H3/11 B3/C4
Craig yr Afon*, Wye Cres..31 D4
Craig yr Haul Drive 30 F1
Crane Street.......................4 F5
Crane Street Mews*, Crane St.
    ....4 F5
Cranham House 8 E6
Crawford Street 14 H6
Crescent Court 16 H2
Crescent Road 16 H2
Crescent, The (Cwmbran) ..8 F6
Crescent, The (Mathern)...32 G1
Cresswell Walk..................7 D5
Crick Road (Portskewett) ..29 B2
Crick Road (Shirenewton) .26 F5
Crindau Road 14 F4
Croeswen 10 G2
Croesyceiliog Bypass.........9 A4
Croft, The 24 F2
Crofton Mede 8 F4
Crofts Corner 7 D5
Cromwell Court.................21 B3
Cromwell Place 9 C1
Cromwell Road (Chepstow)
    ....32 F4
Cromwell Road (Newport) .21 B2
Cross Lane 19 B5
Cross Roads 7 B6

Cross Street (Blaenavon)....1 C4
Cross Street (Caerleon)....16 E4
Cross Street (Garndiffaith) ..2 H1
Cross, The 28 F5
Crossfield Houses 1 C4
Crossway 28 G1
Crossways Close 27 C6
Crouch Close 12 E6
Crown Close (Caerleon) ...15 D4
Crown Close (Cwmbran)....7 B6
Crown Rise 10 E4
Crown Road 10 G4
Crown Street 16 H1
Croydon Close 16 F1
Croydon Court*, Croydon Close
    ....16 F1
Crumlin Road 4 H1
Crumlin Street 4 G5
Cumberland Road 16 F1
Cunningham Road 23 B1
Curie Close 13 D3
Curlew Avenue.................28 G5
Curlew Close 21 D6
Curwood 1 C3
Curzon Court 21 A5
Cutter Close.....................16 E2
Cwm Cwddy Drive 17 C2
Cwm Cwddy Lane 17 C2
Cwm Cwddy Villas...........17 C2
Cwm Dylan Close.............17 C2
Cwm Farm Lane...............14 H6
Cwm Lane 12 G4/H5
Cwm Sor Close 5 D5
Cwm y Nant Fields 8 E6
Cwmavon Road (Abersychan)
    ....2 H3
Cwmavon Road (Blaenavon)
    ....1 C4
Cwmbran Drive
    .....6 H2/9 C1/10 F2/13 A2
Cwmffrdwr Cottages...........2 H3
Cwmffrnwd Square.............2 H3
Cwmffrwdoer......................4 F1
Cwmnant Villas................10 E1
Cwmynyscoy Road.....4 H5/5 D1
Cwr Drive 6 H2
Cwrdy Close 6 F1
Cwrdy Lane........................6 F1
Cwrdy Road 6 F1
Cwrt Bleddyn 8 F6
Cwrt Bleddyn Lane*, Cocker Av.
    ....8 F6
Cwrt Dowlais 10 G1
Cwrt Glas...........................9 C4
Cwrt Morgan 26 G4
Cwrt Pencraig*, Caerau Cres.
    ....19 B3
Cwrt Severn 28 G3
Cypress Close..................15 D1
Cyril Street.......................19 A6
D
D Row.................................1 C2
Daffodil Court.....................8 E3
Daffyn Court.......................2 G2
Daisy Walk..............4 G6/5 C1
Dale Path 8 E4
Dale Road 16 H5
Dancarga Drive 28 F5
Dancing Close 27 B4
Dancing Hill 27 B4
Danes Close.....................31 C3
Danes Hill 31 D6
Daniel Place 19 C5
Daniel Street.....................19 C5

Danygraig 9 A3
Darby Close......................12 H4
Darent Close....................12 E6
Darent Road 12 E6
Darent Walk......................12 E6
Darlington Court 16 F1
Dart Road 14 E1
Darwin Drive 13 D3
David Close......................19 D5
David Walk (3) 17 A4
Davies Court (4).................2 G1
Davies Square..................19 C5
Davis Close 4 E5
Davis Court.......................31 B4
Davis Larner Flats*, Walsall St.
    ....21 B1
Davy Close........................13 D3
Dawson Close 23 C2
Dean Court.........................8 G3
Dean Street 16 H1
Deanery Gardens 19 B5
Deans Gardens 31 C2
Deans Hill 31 C3
Deepweir 28 G6
Deepweir Drive 28 G6
Deepweir Gardens 28 G6
Deer Park Lane 12 H3
Deerbrook..........................8 E4
Delius Close (Rogerstone) 12 G3
Delius Close (Newport) 21 A5
Dell View 31 C3
Denbigh Drive 32 F5/G5
Denbigh Road...................16 F1
Denbury Mews 30 G5
Dene Court (24) 3 D3
Denmark Drive 31 D6
Denny View 28 G6
Denton House (4)...............9 C4
Dents Close 16 H6
Dents Hill 16 H6/21 A6
Derby Grove.....................21 C4
Derwent Court 12 E5
Derwent House...................8 E5
Devauden Road 31 A1
Devon Court 15 C2
Devon Place (Abersychan) .3 A1
Devon Place (Newport) 19 A4
Dewsland Park Road 19 B4
Dewstow Close................28 F3
Dewstow Gardens 28 F4
Dewstow Road (Caerwent)
    ....26 H3
Dewstow Road (Caldicot)..28 E2
Dewstow Street 21 B2
Dibdin Close 23 D1
Dickens Drive 19 D1/D2
Dinas Path 8 E4
Dinch Hill 27 B4
Dingle Lane 1 B6
Dingle Road..............4 G6/5 C1
Dingle, The 20 E3
Dinham Road 26 G3
Ditch Hill 28 E5
Docks Way 19 D5/20 E2
Dockwell Terrace 23 D3
Dolphin Street 19 C6
Don Close.........................14 E1
Doralt Close........................8 F2
Doralt Way..........................8 F2
Dorleigh Court 7 B4
Dorset Close....................21 C4
Dorset Crescent 21 C4
Dorstone Walk 10 E3
Dos Cottages*, Queens Hill
    ....14 H4

Dos Road....14 G4	Edmond Road....31 C6	Exeter Road....16 H1	Fields Road (Pontypool)....10 F2	Fowler Street....4 E4
Dowland Close....21 A6	Edward German Crescent 23 C1	Exeter Street....16 H1	Fields View Road....9 B3	Foxwood Close....17 C3
Downing Street....21 B3	Edward Lane....19 B4	Exmouth Place....31 C4	Fieldside Court (22)....3 D3	Foxwood Court*, Foxwood Cl.
Downside Res. Home....23 D1	Edward Street (Griffithstown)	**F**	Fifth Street....22 F4	....17 C3
Drake Close....23 C1	....6 E2	Factory Lane....3 A2	Filey Road....14 F6	Francis Close....19 C5
Drayton Court....8 E6	Edward Street (Pontypool)..4 F4	Factory Road....14 H4	Finchway Court (8)....2 F2	Francis Drive....19 C5
Drill Hall Street*, Kemys St..6 F2	Edward VII Avenue....19 A2	Fair Bank....1 B3	Fir Tree Close....16 E1	Francis Morris Estate....1 C5
Drinkwater Gardens....19 C2	Edward VII Crescent....19 A3	Fair View....31D2	Fir Tree Cottages....27 C4	Francis Street....19 C5
Drybrook Close....9 D2	Edward VII Lane....19 A3	Fair View Terrace....2 H1	Firbank Avenue....16 G2	Frank Street....14 H5
Duckpool Road....16 G1	Edwin Street (Newport)....14 G5	Fairfax Road....1 B3	Firbank Crescent....16 G3	Fred Edwards Close....23 D1
Dudley Street....21 B1	Edwin Street (Rogerstone)17 B4	Fairfield (Penperlleni)....5 A5/B5	Firs Road....28 E4	Frederick Mews*, Frederick St.
Duffryn Close....17 B3	Eight Houses....3 B2	Fairfield (Talywain)....3 A2	Firs, The (Abersychan)....2 H3	....19 C6
Duffryn Drive....20 F1	Eisteddfod Walk....16 G6	Fairfield Close (Caerleon).15 C2	Firs, The (Blaenavon)....1 C5	Frederick Street....19 C6
Duffryn Lane....18 G5	Elaine Crescent....16 G2	Fairfield Close (Caldicot)...28 F3	Firs, The (Little Mill)....6 H5	Freeholdland Road....3 C3
Duffryn Villas....15 A5	Elan Close....14 E2	Fairfield Road (Caerleon)..15 C2	Firs, The (Newport)....13 D5	Freshwater Road....21 D5
Duffryn Way....20 G1	Elan Walk....8 E5	Fairfield Road (Chepstow) 32 E3	First Street....22 E3	Friars Court....19 B4
Duke Street (Blaenavon)....1 B4	Elan Way....28 E5	Fairfield Terrace....4 E3	Firtree Cottages....4 H6	Friars Crescent....19 B4
Duke Street (Newport)....19 C6	Elder Close....15 D2	Fairfields (Pontypool)....3 C3	Fisher Close....23 B1	Friars Garden....10 F4
Dumfries Place....19 B6	Elgam Avenue....1 A4/B4	Fairhill....8 E4	Fishermans Walk....32 F5	Friars Road....19 C4
Dunlin Avenue....28 G5	Elgam Green (1)....1 B4	Fairhill Walk....8 E4	Fitzosborn Close....31 D3	Friars Street....19 B4
Dunn Square*, Alma St...19 C5	Elgar Avenue....21 A5	Fairoak Avenue....16 H1	Fitzwalter Road....28 G4	Frobisher Road....21 B3
Dunnet Gardens....6 E5	Elgar Circle....21 A5	Fairoak Court....16 H1	Five Houses (Garndiffaith)..2 G1	Frome Walk....11 D6
Dunraven Road....10 E4	Elgar Close....21 A5	Fairoak Grove....17 C2	Five Houses (Pontypool)....4 H4	Frondeg....5 B5
Dunstable Road....21 A6	Elizabeth Sparks Close..28 G1	Fairoak Lane....9 C4	Five Lanes Cottages....25 C6	Fulford Cottages*, Victoria Av.
Dunvagon....30 H3	Elled Road....4 E4	Fairoak Mews....16 H1	Five Locks Close....7 A6	....16 H1
Durand Road....28 G5	Ellick Street....1 B4	Fairoak Terrace....16 H1	Five Locks Road....7 A6/9 A1	**G**
Durham Lane....14 G6	Ellipse, The....6 G1	Fairview Court*, George St. 3 D3	Five Oaks Lane....9 B3	Gables, The*, Bridge Street
Durham Road....16 G1	Ellwood Path....8 E5	Fairwater Close....8 E4	Flats, The....31 D6	....31 B4
Dyffryn Cottages*, Bluetts Road	Elm Avenue....27 C5	Fairwater Square....8 F4	Fleetwood Close....21 B2	Gaer Lane....19 C4
....2 H1	Elm Close (Chepstow)....31 A5	Fairwater Way....8 F4	Fleming Close....13 D3	Gaer Park Avenue....19 C1
Dyke Row....3 D4	Elm Close (Pontypool)....3 C4	Fairway Close....12 G3	Flint Close....16 G3	Gaer Park Drive....19 C1
Dynevor Close....10 E4	Elm Close (Underwood)....23 D5	Fairway,The....5 D4	Flint Court....15 C2	Gaer Park Hill....19 C1
E	Elm Grove (Newport)....13 D4	Falcon Close....28 G5	Florence Place....6 F2	Gaer Park Lane....19 C1
E Row....1 C2	Elm Grove (Pontypool)....6 G2	Fallowfield (6)....8 F5	Foley House (6)....9 C4	Gaer Park Parade....19 C1
Eagle Close....28 G5	Elm Hurst Close....3 C4	Fallowfield Drive....21 C5	Folly Lane....3 D5/D6	Gaer Park Road....19 C1
Earl Close....2 G1	Elm Road (Caldicot)....28 F4	Faraday Close....13 D3	Folly Road....3 D5	Gaer Road....19 C2/C3
Earl Street....2 H1	Elm Road (Chepstow)....31 A5	Farlays....8 F4	Folly View (Pontnewynydd).3 D2	Gaer Street....19 C3
Earlesmede....7 D4	Elmdale....31 B4	Farlow Walk....8 E6	Folly View (Pontypool)	Gaer Vale....19 D2
Earlswood Road....26 F5	Elms Hill....27 B6	Farm Hill....3 D4	....4 E6/5 A1	Gainsborough Close....10 G3
East Avenue....6 G2	Elms, The....31 C6	Farm Lane (Newport)....16 G1	Folly View (Upper Race)....4 H4	Gainsborough Drive....16 F2
East Bank Road....22 E2	Elysia Street....14 G6	Farm Lane (Pontypool)....9 C2	Ford Farm Lane....24 H2	Gainsborough Parc....31 C2
East Dock Cottages....22 F2	Emlyn Road....2 H1	Farm Road (British)....2 H1	Ford Street....19 A5	Garage Cottages....31 A1
East Dock Road....19 B6/21 C1	Emlyn Square....19 A5	Farm Road (Pontypool)....4 G5	Fordwich Close....31 B1	Garden City Way....31 C4
East Grove Road....21 A4	Emlyn Street....19 B5	Farmfield Lane....22 H6	Forest Close (Cwmbran)....8 G4	Gardens, The....27 B3
East Lynne Gardens....15 C4	Emlyn Terrace....2 H1	Farmfield Road....22 H6	Forest Close (Newport)....16 H2	Garn Road....1 A1
East Market Street....19 B6	Emlyn Walk....19 B5	Farmwood Close....16 H4	Forest View....8 G2	Garn yr Erw....1 A1
East Road....10 G2	Empire Terrace....2 G1	Farnaby Close....16 H6	Forge Close....15 C4	Garndyrus Mount....1 A4
East Roedin....8 G5	Endyings (5)....8 F5	Faulkner Road....19 A4	Forge Cottages....15 C4	Garth Close (Newport)....17 C3
East Street....19 A4	Enfield Court*, Caerau Rd.19 B3	Feering Street....21 B1	Forge Gardens....31 B1	Garth Close (Pontypool)....3 C4
East Usk Road....14 H5	Ennerdale Court....16 F2	Fenner Brockway Close...16 G6	Forge Hammer Flats*,	Garth Hill....17 C3
East View (Abersychan)....3 A2	Enterprise Way....19 C6	Fern Court....32 F5	Burford Road....1 B4	Garth Road....8 F6
East View (Griffithstown)....6 F2	Enville Close....8 E4	Fern Rise....13 D4	Forge Lane (Newport)....17 C5	Garth Terrace....17 C3
East View (Pontypool)....4 F5	Enville Road....19 B1	Fernbank....8 E4	Forge Lane*, George St....4 F5	Garthalan Drive....28 H3
East Way Road....20 E6	Eric Coates Walk....21 A6	Ferncroft Way....3 C5	Forge Mews....17 C5	Garthfield Cottages....17 C2
Eastfield Close....15 B3	Eridge Road....2 H2	Ferney Cross....28 F3	Forge Road (Blaenavon)....1 C2	Garvey Close....32 G5
Eastfield Drive....15 B3	Eschol Close....21 B4	Fernhill....10 G5	Forge Road (Newport)....17 D5	Garw Row....9 B4
Eastfield Mews....15 B3	Eschol Court....21 B4	Fernleigh Road....28 F4	Forge Row (Caldicot)....29 D1	Garw Wood Drive....9 B3
Eastfield Road....15 C3	Esperanto Way*, Hathaway St.	Fernside*, Liswerry Rd....21 B5	Forge Row (Pontypool)....4 E3	Garw, The....9 B4
Eastfield View....15 C3	....21 B2	Ferry Way....32 F6	Forgeside Road....1 C3	Gaskell Street....21 B2
Eastfield Way....15 C3	Essex Court....15 C3	Festival Crescent....6 E5	Forgeside*, Taliesin....9 C1	Gatlas Road....15 A4
Eastgate Crescent....26 G3	Essex Street....21 A1	Fetty Place....10 F1	Fort Lea*, Gaer Road..19 C2/C3	Gaudi Walk....12 H3
Eastmoor Road....21 C5	Estate Road....1 A2	Fforest Glade....16 H2	Fort View....17 C3	Gaynors (8)....8 F4
Eastway Road....22 F1/G1	Estuary Road....21 D5	Ffos y Fran....17 C3	Fosse Close....21 C5	Gelli Fawr Court....8 G3
Ebbw Road....28 E5	Estuary View....29 C1	Ffrwd Road....3 A3	Fosse Lane....16 E4	Gelli Place....3 A2
Ebenezer Drive....17 A4	Eton Road....19 A6	Fieldings (7)....8 F5	Fosse Road....21 C5	Gelli Rhwy Road....2 G2
Ebenezer Terrace....19 B5	Evans Street....14 G5	Fields Avenue....9 B1	Foundry Cottages....6 F2	General Rees Square....9 D1
Ebley Gardens*, Pill Rd..28 G6	Evesham Court....14 G4	Fields Park Avenue....19 A2	Foundry Road....3 B2	George Lansbury Drive...16 G6
Ebury House (5)....9 C4	Eveswell Court....21 A1	Fields Park Court*,	Fountain Cottages (1)....31 B1	George Lansbury Home....9 B4
Edgecourt (4)....8 F4	Eveswell Lane*, Eveswell St.	Fields Park Road....19 A2	Fountain Road....5 C2	George Street (Blaenavon).1 C4
Edgehill....10 F5	....21 A2	Fields Park Crescent....19 A2	Fountain Way....32 G5	George Street (Cwmbran)...9 C1
Edinburgh Close (3)....9 B3	Eveswell Park Road....16 H2	Fields Park Gardens....19 A2	Four Ash Court....30 G5	George Street (Newport)...19 B5
Edison Ridge....13 C3	Eveswell Street....21 A2	Fields Park Lane....19 A2	Four Ash Street....30 G5	George Street (Pontnewynydd)
Edlogan Square....9 B3	Exe Road....11 D6	Fields Park Road....19 A2	Four Houses....8 F2	....3 D3
Edlogan Villas....6 G2	Exeter Close....7 D4	Fields Road (Newport)	Fourteen Locks Cottages..12 H5	George Street (Pontypool)
Edlogan Way....9 C2/C3	Exeter Place....3 B2	....14 H4/19 A3	Fourth Street....22 F3	....4 E4/F5

George Street Flats*, George St. 3 D3
Gething Terrace 1 C2
Gibbons Close 21 B5
Gibbs Road.....................21 A3
Gibraltar Way................32 F6
Gibson Lane 4 F5
Gifford Close 8 F6/10 F1
Gilbert Close 21 A6
Gilchrist Thomas Court......1 B3
Gilchrist Walk.........1 B4
Giles Road.....................1 C5
Gileston Walk.............8 E6
Gilwern Farm Close...15 A6
Gilwern Place 7 B6
Glade Close 8 G4
Gladstone Place.........6 G2
Gladstone Terrace (Blaenavon) 1 C4
Gladstone Terrace (Varteg).2 F2
Gladstone Terrace*, Osborne Road..........4 E4
Glan Rhyd 8 G4
Glan y Nant (Cwmbran)....8 F6
Glan y Nant (Llangybi)...24 F2
Glan y Nant Close............8 F6
Glan yr Afon 2 H1
Glanmor Crescent...........16 H4
Glanmor Park Avenue....16 H4
Glansychan Houses......3 A2
Glansychan Lane.........3 A2
Glantorvaen Houses.....1 C3
Glantorvaen Terrace.....4 F5
Glanwern Avenue......16 H5
Glanwern Close..........16 H5
Glanwern Drive 16 H5
Glanwern Grove.......16 H5
Glanwern House (Newport) 16 H5
Glanwern House*, Albion Rd. 4 G4
Glanwern Rise..........16 H5
Glanwern Terrace.......4 G4
Glanyravon Cottages*, Isca Rd. 16 E5
Glascoed Road.........5 D5
Glasllwch Crescent........17 A5
Glasllwch Lane........17 C6
Glasllwch View...........17 C6
Glaslyn Court..........9 B3
Glassworks Cottages...14 F5
Glastonbury Close (2)......14 H5
Glebe Gardens............17 C5
Glebe Street 21 A1
Glen Court*, Monnow Way13 D1
Glen Usk View..........15 B3
Glen View (Chepstow)...32 G1
Glen View (Cwmbran).....7 D6
Glen View (Garndiffaith)....2 H2
Glen, The*, Old Chepstow Rd. 23 A5
Glencourt.........6 G2
Glengariff Court 6 F1
Glenside 7 B6
Glenview Road............3 C4
Gloster Place 14 H6
Gloster Street 14 H6
Glosters Parade 6 E5
Gloucester Close......9 D4
Gloucester Court......15 C3
Gloucester Road........31 A5
Glycoed Way.............28 E5
Glyn View 4 G2
Glyndwr Road 9 D2
Glyntirion..............8 F6

Godfrey Road (Cwmbran)...9 B1
Godfrey Road (Newport)...19 A4
Gold Tops....................19 A4
Goldcliff Court...............10 E2
Goldcliff House*, Goldcliff Ct. 10 E2
Goldcroft Common.......15 D4
Goldcroft Court (2) 15 D4
Goldfinch Close...........28 G4
Goodrich Court (3)........10 E4
Goldsmith Close.........19 D2
Golf Course Lane........12 G3
Golf Road...................5 D4
Golynos Place.........2 H1
Golynos Road.........2 G1
Golynos*, Castlewood.......2 H1
Goodrich Crescent.....14 G4
Goodrich Grove.........20 H1
Goodrich Lane 14 G4
Goossens Close........23 C2
Gordings.................7 D4
Gordon Road............3 A2
Gordon Street..........21 A1
Gore Street...............14 G6
Govilon Place.............7 B6
Gower Green...........9 B3
Goya Close..............16 G3
Grafton Lane.............14 H6
Grafton Road..........19 A5
Graham Bell Close.....13 C2
Graham Street.........19 B4
Grahamstown Grove....31 C6
Grahamstown Road....31 C6
Graig Close.................17 B3
Graig Park Avenue.....14 E4
Graig Park Circle.......14 E3
Graig Park Hill..........14 E4
Graig Park Lane.......14 E4
Graig Park Parade.....14 E4
Graig Park Road........14 E4
Graig Park Villas........14 E4
Graig Road.................7 D3
Graig View..............7 B4
Graig View Terrace.......2 H1
Graig Wood Close.......14 E4
Graigddu View..........2 G1
Grange Cottages......16 E5
Grange Court (27) (Pontypool) 3 D4
Grange Court (Newport)....19 B3
Grange Lane.............9 C1
Grange Park............31 A1
Grange Path.............10 F4
Grange Road (Cwmbran) 9 C2/10 E2
Grange Road (St. Arvans).31 B1
Grange Road (Undy)......27 B4
Granston Houses*, Granston Square......8 E5
Granston Square............8 E5
Granville Close..........17 A5
Granville Lane...........19 B6
Granville Square........19 B6
Granville Street..........19 B6
Granville Terrace........31 B5
Grasmere Way.........32 G5
Great Oaks Park......12 G3
Green Acre.............10 F1
Green Avenue........28 F4
Green Close...........28 G1
Green Cottages.........1 A2
Green Court (Caldicot)...28 G4
Green Court (Cwmbran)....9 B3
Green Farm Cottages...28 E1
Green Fields.............2 G2

Green Lane 28 G4
Green Meadow..............3 A1
Green Moor Lane 27 C2
Green Street (Chepstow)..31 D4
Green Street (Redwick)....27 D1
Green, The.................4 F3
Greene Close.............23 D2
Greenfield (Caerleon)...15 C2
Greenfield (Caldicot).....28 F5
Greenfield Close...........7 A6
Greenfield Cottages (5)...2 G1
Greenfield Place...........1 C4
Greenfield Road.........17 A5
Greenfield Terrace........2 F1
Greenfields View.........24 H5
Greenforge Way.....7 C6/D5
Greenhill................9 C1
Greenhill Close...........6 G2
Greenhill Cottages......9 C1
Greenhill Road (Cwmbran).9 C1
Greenhill Road (Pontypool).6 F2
Greenland Cottages.....3 D1
Greenlands...............3 C1
Greenlands Road........3 D4
Greenmeadow Avenue....21 B5
Greenmeadow Close (Parc-Seymour).......24 E6
Greenmeadow Close (Cwmbran)...........8 E6
Greenmeadow Cottages (Caerleon)..........15 B3
Greenmeadow Cottages (Cwmbran)............7 D5
Greenmeadow Crescent....6 H6
Greenmeadow Drive....24 F6
Greenmeadow House....8 E6
Greenmeadow Road....21 B4
Greenmeadow Square....8 E6
Greenmeadow Way.....7 D5
Greenway...................2 H1
Greenway Close..........6 F1
Greenway Drive.........6 F1
Greenway Walk........6 F1
Greenways, The........27 C3
Greenwich Road........19 D4
Greenwillows...........10 G2
Greenwood Avenue....7 B5
Greenwood Drive......8 G2
Greenwood Flats*, Beaufort Rd. 16 F2
Greenwood Road.......2 H2
Grenadier Drive........23 A4
Grenville Terrace.......28 G2
Grey Waters.............9 D3
Greyhill View.............29 C2
Greys Road...............4 H5
Griffin Avenue.............1 C4
Griffin Court*, Osborne Rd..4 E5
Griffin Street............19 A5
Griffin, The.................17 C4
Griffiths Court...........1 C2
Griffiths Way.............2 H2
Grindle Walk..............12 H3
Groes Close...........12 G4
Groes Road........12 G3/G4
Grosmont Place............9 A3
Grosmont Road..........5 D5
Grosmont Way...........20 H1
Grosvenor Place..........6 G2
Grosvenor Road........17 B2
Grove , The*, Church Rd..28 E5
Grove Close..............3 D3
Grove Court*, East Grove Road 21 A4
Grove Crescent..........3 C4

Grove Estate 3 D3
Grove Estate Road.........3 D3
Grove Gardens..............28 F5
Grove Park 9 A1
Grove Park Avenue......9 A1
Grove Park Drive........14 E5
Grove Place (Cwmbran)....9 A1
Grove Place (Pontypool)....6 F2
Grove Road..................3 D3
Grove Terrace (5).........3 D3
Grove, The..................19 B5
Groves Road.............17 B6
Groveside Villas..........3 D3
Gwaenfelin Walk.........1 B4
Gwent Square............9 D2
Gwent Street.............9 D2
Gwentlands Close.......31 D3
Gwentlands Flats.........31 D3
Gwladys Place...........15 C3
Gwy Court.................31 B4
Gwyn Crescent.........2 F2
Gwyndy Road..........27 B5
Gwynllyw................7 B5
Gypsy Lane...............3 D1

H
Haden Street.............4 F4
Hadrian Close...........15 C3
Hafod Close..........15 A2/B6
Hafod Court 19 B3
Hafod Court Road........7 B4
Hafod Gardens......15 A2/B6
Hafod Mews.......15 A2/B6
Hafod Road..............15 A2/B6
Hafren Road.............7 C4
Haisbro Avenue.........16 F1
Haldane Place..........13 D3
Haldens, The (24)........8 F4
Half Pennies Estate.....15 A6
Halle Close.................23 C2
Halstead Street...........21 A1
Hamilton Street..........21 B2
Hammond Drive.........21 B2
Hampden Court..........21 B3
Hampden Road.........21 B3
Hampshire Avenue.....21 C4
Hampshire Close........21 C4
Hampshire Crescent....21 C4
Hampton Place...........4 E5
Hanbury Close (Caerleon)16 E5
Hanbury Close (Cwmbran)..9 C1
Hanbury Gardens.......3 D3
Hanbury Road (Pontnewynydd) 4 E2
Hanbury Road (Pontypool)..4 F5
Hand Farm Road........4 F5
Handel Close..............23 C2
Handsworth Street.......21 B2
Hanfield Park.............9 C3
Hanley Path...............8 E6
Hanover Close...........31 B2
Hanover Court...........31 C5
Harding Avenue.........13 C3
Hardwick Avenue.......31 D4
Hardwick Hill.............31 D3
Hardwick Hill Lane......31 D3
Hardwick Terrace........31 C3
Hardy Close...............19 D2
Hardy Court (26).........3 D4
Hargreaves Drive.......13 C3
Harlech Close.............9 A3
Harlech Drive............17 B2
Harlequin Court.........14 G4
Harlequin Drive..........14 H4
Harold Street.............9 B1
Harold Walk (4)..........17 A4

Harpers Road..............2 H2
Harrhy Street 19 A5
Harrogate Road...........16 F1
Harrow Close...........15 C2
Harrow Road............19 A6
Hart Gardens*, Alma St...19 C5
Hartridge Farm Road.......23 D1
Harvey Close..............13 D3
Harwood House*, Ty Box Rd. 9 C1
Hassocks Lea (9).........8 F5
Hathaway Street.........21 B2
Hatherleigh.............16 H4
Havelock Street.........19 A5
Haven, The................5 B5
Hawarden Green (4).....10 E4
Hawarden Road.........21 A3
Hawke Close..............23 B1
Hawkes Ridge...........8 F2
Hawkins Crescent.......23 B1
Hawksmoor Close 12 H4
Hawksworth Grove.......21 B4
Hawthorn Close (Chepstow) 32 F4
Hawthorn Close (Underwood) 23 D5
Hawthorn Court..........9 C3
Hawthorn Road...........6 G1
Hawthorn Avenue.......21 A3
Hawthorne Close (Undy)..27 B4
Hawthorne Fosse.......21 A4
Hawthorne Square.....21 A3
Hawthorns, The (Caerleon) 15 A4
Hawthorns, The (Cwmbran)7 B5
Hayling Close.............16 G2
Haynes Court*, James St..19 C6
Hayswayn (10)............8 F4
Hazel Avenue............28 F4
Hazel Close.................5 D5
Hazel Road.................23 B2
Hazel Walk (Caerleon)...15 D2
Hazel Walk (Cwmbran)...9 B3
Hazelton Villas............31 D1
Hazlitt Close.............19 D2
Headland, The...........32 G5
Heath Close.............21 C5
Heather Close...........32 F5
Heather Court............8 F2
Heather Road...........16 F1
Hedgeley Houses*, Llanover Rd. 1 C5
Heidenheim Drive.......14 F5
Helford Square.........11 D6
Helpstone Terrace......4 F3
Hendre Court............8 G3
Hendre Farm Court.....23 B1
Hendre Farm Drive 21 A6/23 B1/D1
Hendre Farm Gardens...23 D1
Hendrew Lane...........24 F5
Hendrick Drive.........31 C5
Henllys Lane (Cwmbran)...8 G2
Henllys Lane (Newport) 11 B1/12 E4
Henllys Way...8 G3/G5/10 F1
Henry Morgan Close....20 G2
Henry Wood Close......21 A5
Henry Wood Walk......21 A5
Hensol Close (Cwmbran)..10 E3
Hensol Close (Rogerstone) 12 G4
Henson Street..........21 B2
Heol Beuno................5 C3
Heol Deiniol...............5 C3

Heol Derwen....5 D4
Heol Glaslyn....28 E5
Heol Isaf....5 D4
Heol Madoc....5 D4
Heol Newydd....7 B5
Heol Padarn....5 D4
Heol Pont y Cwcw....20 G3
Heol Teilo....5 D4
Heol Towy....28 E6
Heol Waun....2 H1
Heol y Pwca....7 B5
Herbert Close....30 H3
Herbert Place....1 C3
Herbert Road....28 E4
Herbert Street....19 B5
Herbert Walk....19 C5
Herberts Close....2 G1
Herberts Road....2 G1
Hereford Court....15 C3
Hereford Street....14 H6
Heron Road....28 G6
Heron Way....20 F3
Heronston Close....27 C6
Hertford Place....16 G2
Heston Close....29 B4
High Bank....16 F1
High Beech Lane....31 D2/D3
High Close....10 F4
High Cross Close....17 B5
High Cross Drive....17 A5
High Cross Lane....17 A5/B5
High Cross Road....17 A5
High Meadow....1 D2
High Street (Abersychan)....3 A1
High Street (Blaenavon)....1 C3
High Street (Caerleon)....15 D4
High Street (Chepstow)....31 C4
High Street (Garndiffaith)....2 G1
High Street (Griffithstown)....6 E2
High Street (Newport)....19 A5
High Street (Pontypool)....4 F4/F5
High View....31 C3
Highcroft Road....14 H3
Highfield (Caerwent)....26 H3
Highfield (Penperlleni)....5 A5
Highfield Close (Caerleon)15 C2
Highfield Close (Pontypool) 3 D2
Highfield Court....17 C3
Highfield Gardens....17 C3
Highfield Lane....17 C3
Highfield Road (Bassaleg) 17 C4
Highfield Road (Caerleon) 15 C2
Highfield Road (Newport)..19 C2
Highfield Way....15 C2
Highland Grove....9 A1
Highmoor Hill....28 E2
Highway, The....6 E4
Highway, The (Croesyceiliog)
....9 B4/C4
Highway, The (Cwmbran)..10 G2
Highway, The (Pontypool)
....5 C2/6 B4
Hill Barn View....29 B4/C3
Hill Brow....32 E1
Hill Crest*, High Street....4 F5
Hill Grove....4 E4
Hill Street (Blaenavon)....1 C4
Hill Street (Cwmbran)....10 F1
Hill Street (Griffithstown)....6 E2
Hill Street (Newport)....19 B5
Hill Street (Pontypool)....3 D3
Hill Top....10 E1
Hill View Crescent....21 C4
Hilla Road....19 A3
Hillcrest (Caerleon)....16 E5

Hillcrest (Garndiffaith)....2 G2
Hillcrest (New Inn)....5 D5
Hillcrest Road....5 C3
Hillrise....2 H2
Hillside....31 A1
Hillside Avenue....1 B4
Hillside Cottages (Panteg)...6 F1
Hillside Cottages (Shirenewton)
....26 E6
Hillside Court....9 C1
Hillside Crescent....17 A5
Hillside Drive....4 H5
Hillside Road....6 E1
Hillstone Place....9 B2
Hilltop....31 D2
Hilltop Green....7 B6
Hillview*, Gaer Rd.....19 C2/C3
Hinter Path (11)....8 F5
Hitchen Hollow....32 G6
Hobart Close....19 B1
Hocker Hill Street....31 C4
Hodges Close....29 B4
Hodges Terrace....7 D6
Hogarth Close (Cwmbran) 10 G3
Hogarth Close (Newport)..16 G2
Holbein Road....16 G3
Holland Close....12 G3
Hollies, The....30 H3
Hollins Close....32 H4
Holly Close....32 F4
Holly Lane....24 H5
Holly Lodge Close....9 B4
Holly Lodge Gardens....9 B4
Holly Lodge Green....9 B4
Holly Lodge Nursing Home .8 F6
Holly Lodge Road....9 B4
Hollybush Avenue....14 E3
Hollybush Close (Cwmbran)8 F6
Hollybush Close (Newport)14 E3
Hollybush Corner....8 F6
Hollybush Cottages*,
Newport Road....6 H4
Hollybush Road....8 G6
Hollybush Terrace....3 D3
Hollybush View....8 G6
Hollybush Walk....17 B3
Hollybush Way....8 G6
Holmdale....8 E4
Holst Close....23 C2
Holyoake Terrace (8)
(Pontypool)....3 D3
Holyoake Terrace*,
Snatchwood Road....3 B3
Home Farm Close....15 D2
Home Farm Crescent....15 D2
Home Farm Green....15 D2
Honddu Close....28 E5
Honeysuckle Close....17 B5
Hood Road....23 B1/B2
Hop Garden, The (4)....32 F5
Hopefield....14 G4
Hopefield Court*, Hopefield
....14 G4
Hopewell Close....32 F5
Hopkins Walk....23 D2
Hornbeam Close....15 D1
Hornbeam Walk....17 C3
Horrocks Close....13 C3
Horseshoe Row....1 D5
Hoskins Street....14 G5
Hospital Road....3 D4
Hospital Villas....10 F5
Hove Avenue....16 G3
Howard Close....23 B1
Howe Circle....23 B1

Howells Row....31 C4
Hubert Rise (5)....17 A4
Hubert Road....16 G1
Hughes Crescent....31 D4
Humber Close....14 E1
Humber Road....14 E1
Hunter Close....12 G4
Hunters Ridge....27 B5
Huntfield Cottages....31 C3
Huntfield Road....31 C2
Huntingdon Close....7 D4
Huxley Green....13 D3
Hydrangea Close....17 B5
Hynam Place....2 H2
I
Ifor Hael Road....12 H3
Ifton Avenue....28 G2
Ifton Lane....27 G2
Ifton Place....21 B3
Ifton Road....28 G2
Ifton Street....21 B3
Ifton Terrace....28 G2
Imperial House....18 G6
Imperial Way....18 G6
Incline Lane....8 F2
Incline Road....A3
Incline Row....2 E2
Incline View....2 H2
Industrial Estate Road....4 E2
Ingles (12)....8 F5
Inner Loop Road....32 E6
Isca Close....9 C2
Isca Court....15 D3
Isca Mews....15 D5
Isca Road....16 E5
Itchen Close....11 D6
Itchen Road....13 D1
Itton Road....31 B2
Ivor Gardens....1 C4
Ivor John Walk....15 B3
Ivor Street (Blaenavon)....1 C4
Ivor Street (Newport)....19 B5
Ivy Cottages (Chepstow)...31 B6
Ivy Cottages*, Viaduct Rd..2 H2
Ivy Dene Close....3 C4
Ivy Road....19 A3
J
Jackson Court....16 H1
Jackson Place....16 H1
James Street (Newport)...19 C6
James Street (Pontypool)
....4 E6/5 A1
James Street (Rogerstone)
....17 A3
Jane Austen Close....19 D2
Jane Close....20 G2
Japonica Close....13 C4
Jasmin Cottages....29 B4
Jeans Close....13 C3
Jeddo Close....19 D5
Jeddo Street....19 C5
Jeffrey Street....21 A1
Jellicoe Close....23 B1
Jenkins Street....21 B2
Jerusalem Close....6 E5
Jerusalem Lane....6 E5
Jervis Walk....23 B1
Jessop Close....12 H4
Jessop Road....12 H4
Jewell Lane....14 F4
Jim Crow Square....9 C4
John Baker Close....10 G2
John Bull Close....16 H6
John Field Walk....21 A6
John Frost Square....19 A5

John Ireland Close....21 A6
John Street (Newport)....19 B6
John Street (Pontypool)....4 G5
Johnston Close....12 G4
Jolyons Court....28 F6
Jones Street....19 B4
Joyce Close....19 C1
Jubilee Place*, Viaduct Rd..2 H2
Jubilee Terrace....4 E4
Jubilee Way....28 F5
Jule Road....8 F5
Julius Close....15 C2
Junction Road....14 H6
Juniper Crescent....8 G3
K
Kears Row....2 E2
Keats Close (Cwmbran)....8 E6
Keats Close (Newport)....19 D1
Keene Avenue....17 B5
Keene Street....21 B2
Keer Street....19 B5
Keir Hardie Crescent....16 G6
Keir Hardie Drive....16 G6
Kelly Road....16 G3
Kelvedon Street....21 B1
Kelvin Close....13 D3
Kemys Fawr Close....6 G1
Kemys Street....6 F2
Kemys Walk....8 F6
Kenfig Place....10 E3
Kendall Square....31 C4
Kenilworth Place....8 F6
Kenilworth Road....21 A3
Kennard Court....1 C3
Kennard Crescent....1 B3
Kennard Place....1 B3
Kennet Grange....24 F2
Kensington Gardens....16 H2
Kensington Grove....21 A2
Kensington Park....27 C3
Kensington Place....16 H2
Kent Close....12 G3
Kent Court....15 C3
Kestrel Close....28 G5
Kestrel Way....20 F1
Keynsham Avenue....19 B5
Kidwelly Close....10 E4
Kidwelly Road....10 E4
Kiln Way....27 B5
Kimberley Terrace....14 F4
King Alfreds Road....31 D6
King Street (Blaenavon)....1 B3
King Street (Newport)....19 B5
King Street (Pontypool)....4 F4
Kingfisher Close....28 G5
Kingfisher Place....20 F1
Kings Hill Court*, Stow Hill 19 B3
Kings Lane....19 B5
Kings Parade....19 C6
Kingsacre....19 A3
Kingsdale Court....19 B3
Kingsland Walk....7 D5
Kingslea (13)....8 F5
Kingsmark Lane....31 B2
Kingsmill Lane*, Clyffard Cres.
....19 A4
Kingsmill Terrace....19 A4
Kingston Road....21 A1
Kingsway....19 A5/B5
Kingsway Centre....19 B5
Kinnock Court....9 B3
Kipling Hill....19 C1
Kipling Road....28 F3
Kirby Daniel Court....19 C5

Kirby Lane....19 C5
Kirrlach Close....28 F3
Kitchener Street....4 E2
Kitty Hawk Drive....21 C3
Knight Close*, Francis Dr..19 C5
Knighton Court....15 D4
L
Laburnam Close....12 G1
Laburnam Close....27 B5
Laburnam Cottages (Chepstow)
....31 A1
Laburnam Grove....29 B4
Laburnam Terrace....29 B4
Laburnam Way....32 E3
Laburnam Cottages (Caeleon)
....5 D5
Laburnam Drive (Cwmbran)8 G3
Laburnam Drive (Newport)21 A3
Laburnam Drive (Pontypool)
....5 D5
Laburnam Gardens....24 H5
Lady Bench....8 F4
Lady Margaret Court (2) ...32 G4
Ladyhill....30 F6
Ladyhill Close....30 F5
Ladyhill Green....21 A5
Ladyhill Road....21 A5
Ladywell....9 B1
Ladywood....30 F6
Lake Road....22 E5
Lamb Close....19 D1
Lamb Lane....15 A5
Lambert Close....14 G4
Lambert Street....14 G4
Lambourne Crescent....14 E1
Lambourne House....13 D1
Lambourne Walk....12 E6
Lambourne Way....13 D1
Lancaster Road....6 F4
Lancaster Way....31 C2
Landau Close....27 B5
Landing, The....3 B1
Landseer Close....16 G3
Langham House....32 E4
Langland Way....21 D3
Langley Close....27 B3
Langstone Cottages....23 A3
Langstone Court....8 F5
Langstone Court Road....23 B4
Langstone Lane....23 C4
Lansdown Terrace*,
Llanover Road....1 C5
Lansdowne....6 G2
Lansdowne Road (Caerleon)
....15 D4
Lansdowne Road (Newport)
....19 C2
Lapwing Avenue....28 G6
Larch Close....5 D5
Larch Court....15 D3
Larch Grove (Newport)13 C4/D4
Larch Grove (Underwood) 23 D5
Larkfield Avenue....31 D3
Larkfield Close....15 C2
Larkfield House*, Larkfield Park
....31 D3
Larkfield Park....31 D3
Larkhill Close....31 D3
Lasgarn Lane....2 H5/3 A4
Lasgarn Place....3 B3
Lasgarn View (Garndiffaith) 2 H2
Lasgarn View (Varteg)....2 F2
Lasgarn Villas....3 A3
Latch Square*, Alma St.....19 C5

Laurel Close 27 B5
Laurel Crescent (Newport)
..........................13 D4
Laurel Crescent (Undy) 27 C5
Laurel Drive (Newport) 17 C4
Laurel Drive (Penperlleni) ...5 A5
Laurel Green.....................7 B5
Laurel Park 31 B1
Laurel Road....................17 B2
Laurel Walk*, Laurel Grn. ...7 B5
Laurels, The..................26 E6
Lavender Way.................12 G1
Lavery Close 16 G3
Lawns, The (Usk) 30 G5
Lawns, The (Magor) 27 C3
Lawrence Court*,
      Lawrence Hill Av. 21 A4
Lawrence Crescent 26 G3
Lawrence Hill 16 H4/21 A3
Lawrence Hill Avenue 21 A3
Laybourne Close 9 C1
Lea Close (Newport) 14 E1
Lea Close (Undy) 27 B4
Leach Road...................11 C5
Leadon Court....................7 C4
Leas, The 7 B5/B6
Ledbrook Close 8 F6
Ledbury Street................14 H5
Lee Way...........21 C5/22 E5
Leechpool Holdings.........29 A4
Leeway Court..................21 D5
Leicester Drive 7 D4
Leicester Road...............16 H1
Leigh Road......................3 C3
Leighton Court..................8 E6
Lennard Street................21 A1
Leslie Green Court 20 E2
Leslie Terrace (6) 17 A4
Lethbridge Terrace 3 B2
Lewis Close (Garndiffaith)...2 G1
Lewis Close (Newport) 19 C5
Lewis Road......................3 D2
Lewis Street.....................3 A2
Lewis Terrace 3 D4
Lewis View (7) 17 A4
Lewis Way....................32 G5
Leybourne Houses........30 G5
Libeneth Road...............21 B3
Lighthouse Park Estate 20 F2
Lighthouse Road 20 E2
Lilburne Drive 21 B2
Lilleshall Street 21 B1
Lime Close 19 D5
Lime Crescent 21 B4
Lime Grove 23 A5
Limekiln Road..................3 C3
Limes, The (Undy) 27 B4
Lincoln Close................16 H2
Lincoln Court 15 C3
Lindbergh Close 21 C3
Linden Close.................32 F3
Linden Court....................8 F5
Linden Road 21 A3
Link Road........................5 D4
Links, The........................3 C5
Linley Close 23 C2
Linnet Road..................28 G5
Linton Court......................3 B3
Linton Street.................19 C6
Lion Court........................1 B4
Lion Street.......................1 B4
Liscombe Street 21 B2
Lister Green...................13 D3
Liswerry Close (5) 10 E4
Liswerry Drive 9 D4/10 E4

Liswerry Park Drive 21 B5
Liswerry Road 21 A5/B4/B5
Little Innage Barns 32 H2
Little Oaks View 12 G3
Littledene 8 E4
Livale Close 13 D2
Livale Court 13 D1
Livale Road 13 D2
Livale Walk 13 D1
Liverpool Street..............16 H1
Livingstone Place 21 A1
Llan Honddu 3 B3
Llanarth Street 19 A5
Llandaff Green.................9 C2
Llandaff Street...............19 C4
Llandegfedd Close 12 G4
Llandegfedd Way..............6 E4
Llandegveth Close............9 B4
Llandenny Walk.............10 E2
Llanderfel Court................7 C4
Llandowlais Street 10 F1
Llanerch Close.................4 E4
Llanerch Path 8 E5
Llanfoist Crescent 1 B4/B5
Llanfrechfa Way.............10 E2
Llangattock Court 9 B4
Llangorse Drive 12 G4
Llangorse Path 10 F3
Llangorse Road 10 E3
Llanon House 9 A2
Llanover Close (Newport) .14 E3
Llanover Close*, Llanover Road
....1 C5
Llanover Road (Blaenavon) 1 C4
Llanover Road (Varteg).......2 E3
Llanover Road Estate 1 C5
Llantarnam Bypass.10 H4/13 B4
Llantarnam Close 10 F2
Llantarnam Gardens*,
      Greenwillows 10 G2
Llantarnam House...........10 H2
Llantarnam Park Way 10 H2
Llantarnam Road 10 E2/F2
Llanthewy Close 9 B4
Llanthewy Road 19 B3
Llanthony Close 28 F6
Llanvair Road (Caerwent) .26 F2
Llanvair Road (Newport) ...14 H6
Llanwern Road (Magor) 27 C1
Llanwern Road (Newport) .23 B1
Llanwern Street 21 A1
Llanyravon Square 10 E3
Llanyravon Way..............10 E3
Llew a Dor Court*, Broadwell Ct.
....15 D4
Llewellin Street 21 A3
Llewellyn House 10 E2
Lloyd Street 21 B3
Llwyn Celyn 8 F6
Llwyn Deri Close 17 C2
Llwyn Deri Road 19 A3
Llwyn On (Ponthir) ...15 A3/B6
Llwyn Onn (Cwmbran) 9 C4
Llwyn y Llan Flats............3 D5
Llyn Berwyn Close 12 G4
Llyn Celyn Close 12 G4
Llys Gaer*, Stow Park Crescent
....19 B3
Llys Gwyrdd 8 G3
Llys Tadcu*, Maryport St. 30 G5
Llyswen Walk 10 F3
Llywelyn Road 9 D1
Lock Up Lane 3 B2
Locke Street 14 H4
Lodden Close 14 E1

Lodge Avenue 15 C3
Lodge Hill (Caerleon) 15 C2
Lodge Hill (Llanwern) 23 C4
Lodge Road (Caerleon) ...15 D3
Lodge Road (Talywain) 3 A1
Lodge Way 29 C1
Lodges, The*, Wednesbury St.
....21 B2
Lodgewood 5 C2
Lon Helyg 9 C4
Lon Nant 9 B2
London Street.................16 H1
Long Acre (14) 8 F5
Long Hollow 9 C1
Long Row 4 H4
Longbridge 15 A1/B5
Longcroft Road 28 G4
Longditch Road 21 D6
Longfellow Close............28 G3
Longfellow Court 28 G3
Longfellow Place 28 G3
Longfellow Road 28 G3
Longhouse Barn 5 A5
Longhouse Grove 8 G3
Longmeadow Court 21 B5
Lookout Cottages*, Mounton Rd.
....31 C2
Loop Road 32 E6
Lord Eldon Drive 32 G4
Lord Street 14 H6
Loreto House*, Allt yr Yn Av.
....14 H3
Lower Bridge Street...........4 F5
Lower Church Street 31 B4
Lower Dock Street ..19 B5/B6
Lower Ellick Street*, Ellick St.
....1 B4
Lower Garn Terrace 1 A2
Lower Glantorvaen Terrace 1 C3
Lower Harpers Road........2 H3
Lower Hill Street (7)..........1 C4
Lower Leigh Road*, Leigh Rd.
....3 C3
Lower Market Arcade*,
      Crane Street 4 F5
Lower Park Gardens 4 E5
Lower Park Terrace 4 G5
Lower Pentwyn Cottages.30 H3
Lower Stoney Road..........2 H2
Lower Ty Gwyn Road 2 G2
Lower Waun Street............1 B3
Lower Woodland Street.....1 B4
Lowlands Court 9 B1
Lowlands Crescent...........9 A1
Lowlands Road................9 B1
Lowndes Close 17 B3
Lucas Street 14 H4
Ludlow Close (Cwmbran) .10 F4
Ludlow Close (Newport)....21 B2
Lulworth Road 16 E5
Lundy Drive 16 G2
Lyncroft 7 D4
Lyndhurst Avenue 19 D3
Lyndon Way (8) 17 A4
Lyne Road 14 G5
Lysted House*,
      Greenmeadow Way ...8 E6
M
Macarthys Court.............19 A5
Macaulay Gardens.........19 D2
Machine Meadow 3 D3
Madocke Road 31 D6
Magnetty Place 7 B5
Maendy Square 7 B5
Maendy Way........7 A5/9 C1

Maendy Wood Rise 7 B5
Maerdy Close 19 D3
Maes y Celyn...................5 D1
Maesderwen Crescent.....5 C1
Maesderwen Rise 5 D1
Maesderwen Road...........5 C1
Maesglas Avenue...........19 D3
Maesglas Close 20 E3
Maesglas Crescent.........20 E2
Maesglas Grove 20 E2
Maesglas Road 20 E3
Maesglas Street 23 E3
Maesgwyn 7 A6
Magna Porta Gardens 10 H4
Magnolia Close (Chepstow)
....32 F5
Magnolia Close (Newport) 13 C4
Magor Court....................27 B3
Magor Road 27 A1
Magor Street..................21 B2
Main Road (Magor) 27 C4
Main Road (Portskewett) .29 C3
Maindee Parade 16 H1
Maindee Terrace 7 B6
Major Close 8 E3
Malcolm Sargent Close 21 A6
Mall, The 9 D2
Mallard Avenue 28 G5
Mallard Way 20 G2
Mallards Reach 30 G2
Malmesbury Close (3) 14 H5
Malpas Court 13 C2
Malpas Court Estate........13 D3
Malpas Lane 14 F4
Malpas Road 13 C3/14 E3/F4
Malpas Street..................10 E1
Malthouse Lane (Caerleon)
...........................15 A1/B5
Malthouse Lane (Pontypool)
....4 E4
Malthouse Road ....13 A
Malvern Close (Newport) .16 F2
Malvern Close (Risca).....12 E1
Malvern Road.................19 A6
Manchester Street..14 H6/16 H1
Manley Road 19 B3
Manor Chase..................27 C5
Manor Court (Rogiet) 28 G2
Manor Court (Usk)...........30 H6
Manor Gate 7 D5
Manor Park.....................20 G3
Manor Road 2 H2/3 A1/A2
Manor View....................31 B1
Manor Way (Abersychan) ..3 A2
Manor Way (Chepstow) ...31 C3
Manor Way (Portskewett) .29 C2
Mansel Street 21 A3
Maple Avenue 32 E3/F4
Maple Close (Caldicot) ...28 F4
Maple Close (Underwood) 25 D5
Maple Crescent 6 G1
Maple Road 6 F1
Maple Road South 6 G1
Marconi Close 13 D2
Margaret Avenue 14 G6
Margretts Way................28 F5
Marigold Close 12 G1
Marina Court 16 F1
Marine Terrace 29 C3
Mariner Way 22 E1
Mariners Reach 32 G5
Marion Place 19 D5
Marion Street 19 D5
Market Arcade*, Crane St. ..4 F5

Market Arcade*, High Street
....19 A5
Market Street (Blaenavon)..1 C4
Market Street (Newport) ...19 A5
Market Street (Pontypool) ...4 F5
Market Street Court*, Market St.
....4 F5
Market Street Square*,
      Market Street..............4 F5
Marl Court......................27 C4
Marlborough Road (Cwmbran)
....7 D3
Marlborough Road (Newport)
....19 A6
Marloes Path 7 D4
Marlowe Close 12 H4
Marlowe Gardens 19 D3
Marryat Walk 19 D2
Marsh Road....................32 E4
Marshfield Road 30 E1
Marshfield Street 21 C2
Marston Court 14 G4
Marston Path 8 E5
Marten Road...................32 E4
Martin Close 28 G1
Martin Terrace 1 C2
Martindale Road 6 F2
Martins Road 26 H3
Martins Row 27 C4
Martins, The 31 B5
Mary Street (6) 1 C4
Maryport Street 30 G5
Marysfield Close.............30 H3
Masefield Road 28 G4
Masefield Vale................19 C2
Masie Court 19 C5
Mathern Road 32 G2/E3
Mathern Way 32 E4
Matthew Terrace 3 D3
Maugham Close 19 D2
Maxworthy Row................1 C4
May Cottages 17 A3
May Street 21 A1
Maybury House*, Byways...8 E5
Maynes (15)....................8 F4
McIntyre Court*, Commercial St.
....6 E2
Mead Lane (Cwmbran) 9 C1
Mead Lane (Redwick) 27 D1
Meadow Bank....................5 A5
Meadow Brook Avenue......7 A6
Meadow Close 6 G2
Meadow Croft..................28 G1
Meadow Lane (Chepstow)31 C3
Meadow Lane (Cwmbran) ..9 C4
Meadow Rise 27 B4
Meadow Walk 31 C3
Meadow Way 5 A5
Meadowlands Close 24 F6
Meadows Road...............22 F5
Meadows, The (Magor) ...27 C3
Meadows, The (Marshfield)
....30 G2
Meadows, The (Usk) 30 G6
Meads Close 21 C4
Meads Court 32 E4
Meadway 28 G1
Medlock Close 13 D1
Medlock Crescent 13 D1
Medlock Walk 13 D1
Medway Close 11 D6
Medway Court 11 D6
Medway Road 11 D5
Melbourne Court...............8 E6
Melbourne Way.......17 B6/19 B1

Melfort Gardens 19 C2
Melfort Road 19 B6
Melling Court*, Osborne Rd.4 F5
Mellon Street 19 B6
Melyn Bach Avenue 6 G6
Mendalgief Road 19 C5
Mendip Close 16 H5
Meon Close 13 D2
Merchants Hill 4 E4
Merchants Hill Close 4 E4
Mercian Way 31 D6
Mere Path 7 D4
Meredith Close 19 C3
Merlin Close*, Barn Owl Road
....28 G1
Merlin Crescent 16 G2
Merriotts Place 16 H1
Merrivale Cottages 27 C3
Mersey Walk 12 E6
Merton Green 26 F2
Mervyn Terrace (Pontnewynydd)
....3 D2
Mervyn Terrace (Pontypool)4 E5
Methuen Road 21 A1
Mews, The (Newport) 19 A3
Mews, The*, Crane Street ...4 F5
Mews, The*, Stow Park Circle
....19 B3
Meyricks, The 8 G4
Michael Way 4 E5
Middle Coed Cae 1 C5
Middle Street 31 C4
Middle Way 32 F4
Midfield 5 B5
Milford House*, Farlow Wk..8 E6
Mill Common 27 C4
Mill Heath 13 D1
Mill Lane (Caldicot) 28 G5
Mill Lane (Castleton) 30 E1
Mill Lane (Chepstow) 31 C4
Mill Lane (Cwmbran) 8 G4
Mill Parade 19 D6
Mill Reen 27 B4
Mill Road 3 D4
Mill Street (Caerleon) 15 D4
Mill Street (Newport) 14 H5
Mill Street (Usk) 30 H5
Mill Street Close 30 H5
Millbrook Court (Little Mill) ...6 H6
Millbrook Court (Undy) 27 C4
Millbrook Place 6 H6
Miller Close 24 H2
Millers Ride 10 E3
Millfield Park 27 B4
Milman Street 19 D5
Milner Street 21 B2
Milton Close 8 E6
Milton Court 23 B1
Milton Hill 23 C3
Milton Road 21 A2
Minories (16) 8 F5
Miskin Court 27 C6
Miskin Green 9 D3
Miskin House*, Miskin Green
....9 D3
Mission Hall Road 3 B1
Mitchell Terrace (2) 3 D3
Mithras Way 15 C3
Mobile Homes*, Brynwern..4 F4
Model Cottages (Chepstow)
....32 G1
Model Cottgaes (Sedbury)31 D6
Mole Close 11 D6
Molescombe (17) 8 F5
Mona Close 9 C2

Mona Cottages 30 G5
Monet Crescent 16 G3
Monks Close 28 F5
Monmouth Close 6 E4
Monmouth Crescent 6 F4
Monmouth Drive 16 F3
Monmouth House*,
Monmouth Square 9 D2
Monmouth Road (St. Arvans)
....31 B1
Monmouth Road (Usk)..30 G5
Monmouth Square 9 D2
Monmouth Walk*,
Monmouth Square 9 D2
Monnow Court 7 C3
Monnow Walk 11 D6/12 D6
Monnow Way
..11 D6/12 E6/13 D2/14 E1
Montague Almshouse*,
Upper Church St. 31 C4
Montgomery Road 13 C3
Montreal Close 17 B6
Montresor Court 10 H4
Moor Street 31 C3
Moore Crescent 23 C2
Moorings, The 16 F2
Moorland Avenue 21 B5
Moorland Park 21 B5
Moorlands View 28 G6
Mopla Cottages 31 A5
Mopla Road 31 A4
Morden Lane 16 G1
Morden Road 16 G1
Moreton Street 4 F4
Morgan Rise (2) 1 B4
Morgan Street (Blaenavon).1 C4
Morgan Street (Newport) ..14 G6
Morgan Way 20 G2
Morgraig Avenue 20 G1/H1
Morley Close 21 A6
Morris Rise (3) 1 B4
Morris Street 19 A6/21 A1
Morton Way 19 D2
Moseley Terrace 9 A2
Moss Road 7 D5
Mount Ballan 29 A1
Mount Bax 21 A5
Mount Pleasant (Chepstow)
....31 D3
Mount Pleasant (Newport) 13 D3
Mount Pleasant (Pontnewynydd)
....3 D3
Mount Pleasant (Talywain)..3 A2
Mount Pleasant Close 9 B1
Mount Pleasant Court*,
Nicholas Street.......4 G5
Mount Pleasant Hill 9 B1
Mount Pleasant Road .7 B6/9 B1
Mount Road.........................3 D6
Mount Way 31 B3/C3
Mount, The*, St. Johns Cres.
....4 E3
Mountain Lane 6 E1
Mountain Road (Cwmbran).7 A4
Mountain Road (Risca) ...12 E1
Mountain View Road 3 D3
Mountbatten Close 23 B2
Mountford Close 12 G4
Mountjoy Place 19 B5
Mountjoy Road 19 B5
Mountjoy Street 19 B5
Mounton Close 31 D2
Mounton Drive 31 D2
Mounton Road 31 C2/D1
Mountside 12 E1

Moxon Road 14 E3
Moyle Grove 15 A2/B6
Mulberry Close 12 G1
Mulcaster Avenue 21 C4
Munnings Drive 16 G3
Museum Court*, Museum St.
....15 D4
Museum Street 15 D4
Mynydd Court 4 H5
Mynydd Maen Road 7 A5
Mynydd View 4 H5
Myra Hess Close 23 B2
Myrtle Close 17 B5
Myrtle Cottages 16 E5
Myrtle Drive 17 B5
Myrtle Grove 21 A4
Myrtle Place 16 E5
Myrtles, The 31 B5
N
Nant Celyn Close 7 B5
Nant y Milwr Close 8 G3
Nantcoch Drive 19 A1
Nantymor Cottages 18 G4
Narberth Crescent 10 E4
Nash Close 12 H2
Nash Drive 21 C4
Nash Grove 21 C4
Nash Mead 22 E5
Nash Road ...21 C4/D4/22 F4
Neath Court 7 D4
Neath Villas 3 B2
Neddern Court 28 E4
Neddern Way 28 E4
Neerings 8 F3
Nelson Drive 23 C1
Nelson Street 31 C4
Neston Road 16 H6
Nethercourt (6) 10 E4
Netherwent View 27 B3
Neuadda Close 17 C2
Nevern Walk (6) 10 E4
Neville Street 2 H2
Neville Terrace 1 A4
New Barn Path 10 F4
New Chapel Court*, Waun Rd.
....8 F6
New Cottages (Caerwent) 26 G2
New Cottages*, East Usk Rd.
....14 H5
New Houses (6) (Garndiffaith)
....2 G1
New Houses (Pontypool) ...4 G4
New James Street 1 C4
New Market Street 30 G5
New Pastures 19 C3
New Quay Road 22 E1
New Queen Street 1 B4
New Road (Caerleon) 16 E5
New Road (Caldicot) 28 F4
New Road (Garndiffaith) 2 G1
New Road (Pontypool) 6 E2
New Road (Talywain) 3 A3
New Row 8 F2
New Ruperra Street 19 B6
New Street (Cwmbran) 9 B1
New Street (Newport) 19 C6
New Terrace*, Grove Rd....3 D2
New William Street 1 C4
Newchurch Court 8 E6
Newgale House*, St. Davids Rd.
....9 D2
Newgale Row 10 E2
Newlands Court (12) 3 D3
Newman Close 23 C1
Newman Road 3 C4

Newnham Place 10 E2
Newport Arcade*, High St. 19 A5
Newport Road (Caldicot)
........................28 F3/F5/G4
Newport Road (Castleton)30 E1
Newport Road (Chepstow)
........................31 D2/32 E1
Newport Road (Cwmbran)
....................10 H4/13 B3
Newport Road (Magor).....27 B3
Newport Road (Pontypool)
....................6 G4/H4/9 A4
Newport Road (Pwllmeyric)
....32 E1
Newton Green Cottages...32 F1
Newton Manor 26 F5
Newton Way 13 D3
Newton Wynd (18) 8 F5
Newtown Road 5 B5
Neyland Path (19) 4 F5
Nicholas Street 4 G5
Nidd Close 12 E6
Nidd Walk 12 E6
Nightingale Close 28 G5
Nightingale Court 12 E6
Nightingale House 9 C1
Nightingale Terrace 3 D3
Nile Street 10 F1
Nolton Place 8 F5
Nook, The*, Pisgah Road ...2 H1
Norbury House 8 E6
Norfolk Close 7 D3
Norfolk Road 16 H2
Norman Boult Green 21 B5
Norman Court 28 G5
Norman Street 15 D4
Norman Terrace 15 D4
Norman Way 29 C1
Normands House 8 F5
Normandy Way 31 B2
Norse Way 31 D6
North Court (20) 23 C4
North Road (Abersychan) ...3 B3
North Road (Cwmbran) 9 B3
North Road (Pontypool)......4 F4
North Row 27 D1
North Street (Blaenavon) ...1 B3
North Street (Newport) 19 A5
North View 3 C3
North Walk 9 D2
Northfield Close 15 C2
Northfield Road 15 C2
Northumberland Road......16 H2
Novello Walk 23 D1
O
O'Neal Avenue 22 E3
Oak Bluff 32 E1
Oak Close (Chepstow) 32 F3
Oak Close (Undy) 27 B4
Oak Cottages 26 E6
Oak Court (13) 3 D3
Oak Road 12 H2
Oak Street (Cwmbran) 10 E1
Oak Street (Newport)
........................14 F6/16 F1
Oak Tree Close 5 D4
Oak Tree Court 10 F2
Oak Tree Drive 12 G1
Oak View 1 C5
Oakdale Close 15 D2
Oakdale Path 8 E6
Oakdale Place 3 D3
Oakfield (Caerleon) 15 C2
Oakfield Avenue 31 C2
Oakfield Gardens 19 A3

Oakfield Road (Cwmbran) .10 F2
Oakfield Road (Newport)...19 A3
Oakfield Terrace 1 C4
Oakfields (Marshfield) 30 H2
Oakgrove 31 B1
Oaklands 15 A1/B5
Oaklands Park 29 B2
Oaklands Park Drive 17 C2
Oaklands Road (Newport) 16 H2
Oaklands Road (Pontypool)
....6 G1
Oaklands Terrace 10 G1
Oaklands View 7 D3
Oakleigh Court 8 G2
Oakley Close 28 F3
Oakley Street 21 B2
Oakley Way 28 F4
Oaks Close 19 C3
Oaks Court 3 B7
Oaks Court Estate*, Oaks Court
....3 B2
Oaks Road 3 B2
Oaks, The (Cwmbran).......9 C4
Oaks, The (Llangybi) 24 F2
Oaks, The (Underwood)...23 C5
Oaksford 8 E3
Octagon, The 32 E4
Octavius Close 20 G2
Offas Close 31 D5
Offway 8 G5
Ogmore Crescent 12 E6
Ogmore Place 10 E4
Ogwen House 8 E5
Old Bailey 5 C1
Old Barn Court 27 B6
Old Barn Estate 16 F2
Old Bridge Road 7 B4
Old Bulwark Road 31 D3
Old Cardiff Road 20 E2
Old Chepstow Road 23 A2
Old Chepstow Road 23 A3
Old Estate Yard*, Fountains Rd.
....5 C2
Old Green Court 30 H3
Old Hill (Chepstow) 31 B4
Old Hill (Newport) 16 F5
Old Hill Crescent 16 F5
Old Houses 3 B2
Old James Street 1 C4
Old Lane 3 A2
Old Langstone Court Road
....23 A4
Old Market Street 30 G5
Old Oak Close 32 F5
Old Paddocks 23 A5
Old Penygarn 4 E5
Old Road 3 B3
Old Row (Cwmbran) 8 F2
Old Row (Sudbrook) 29 D4
Old School Place (10) 3 D2
Old Stone Road 27 B5
Old William Street 1 C4
Oldbridge Court 7 B4
Oldbury Road 10 E2
Oliphant Circle 13 C2
Oliver Road 21 B3
Olway Close 10 F4
Ombersley Lane 19 B3
Ombersley Road 19 B2
Open Hearth Close 6 F2
Orchard Avenue 32 E3
Orchard Close (Caldicot) ..28 G4
Orchard Close (Marshfield)
....30 H2
Orchard Close (Newport) ..17 C2

Orchard Close (Pontypool) .3 C4
Orchard Court*, Orchard Street
..................................14 G6
Orchard Farm Close..........31 D6
Orchard Farm Estate..........3 D5
Orchard Gardens (Chepstow)
..................................31 B4
Orchard Gardens (Portskewett)
..................................29 C2
Orchard Lane (Cwmbran) 9 C2
Orchard Lane (Newport)......16 G1
Orchard Mews....................14 G6
Orchard Place 10 E1
Orchard Rise (Chepstow)..32 F1
Orchard Rise (Shirenewton)
..................................26 F5
Orchard Road 15 B3
Orchard Street 14 G6
Orchard, The (Caerleon)
..............................15 A2/B6
Orchard, The*, Church Road
..................................27 C6
Orchid Court 8 F3
Orchid Drive 27 C3
Orchid Meadow 32 F1
Oriel Road 21 A1
Ormerod Road 31 D6
Osborne Close 16 H1
Osborne Flats...................3 C4
Osborne Road............4 E4/E5
Osprey Drive 28 G6
Oswald Road.....................19 D5
Otter Close 11 D6
Owen Close 15 B3
Owendale Terrace..............3 B3
Oxford Close 15 C2
Oxford Street (Chepstow).31 C4
Oxford Street (Newport) 21 A1
Oxford Street (Pontypool) ...6 E2
Oxford Terrace 1 C2
Oxtens..............................8 G5
Oxwich Road 21 D2
P
Pace Road 8 F4
Padarn Place.....................9 C1
Paddock Close 7 B6
Paddock Rise 10 F4
Paddock, The (Chepstow).32 E3
Paddocks, The (Caerleon) 15 C2
Paddocks, The (Cwmbran) 10 F4
Paddocks, The (Undy) 27 B6
Palm Close 5 C5
Palm Square....................21 A3
Palmyra Place 19 B5
Pandy...............................7 D5
Pant Glas Cottages 13 A1
Pant Glas Lane*, Pentre Lane
..................................13 B1
Pant Glas Road 13 A1
Pant Gwyn Close..............8 F3
Pant Lane........................14 F4
Pant Road 14 F4
Pant yr Eos 9 C1
Pant yr Heol Close............8 G3
Panteg Way.......................5 D3
Pantglas............................3 B1
Pantglas Court 17 C2
Parade, The......................9 D2
Parc Avenue.....................9 B1
Parc Close 24 F1
Parc Road 24 F1
Parc y Brain Lane...............5 B5
Parc y Brain Road.............12 F5
Pardoe Thomas Close*,
    Coulson Close..........19 C5

Parfitt Street.....................21 B4
Parfitt Terrace....................7 B6
Park Avenue (Newport).....19 D2
Park Avenue (Rogerstone)12 H2
Park Close (Cwmbran) 8 G2
Park Close (Newport)........20 E2
Park Cottages (Pontypool)..5 B1
Park Cottages*, The Park ..1 B3
Park Court (Undy) 27 C6
Park Court*, Park Road......4 E5
Park Crescent (Newport)...20 E2
Park Crescent (Pontypool)
..............................4 E6/5 A1
Park Drive........................19 D2
Park End..........................23 A5
Park End Court*, Pk. End..23 A5
Pendine Walk.....................8 E5
Pendoylan Walk..................8 F6
Penkin Close 21 A6
Penkin Hill.......................21 A6
Penllyn Avenue (Cwmbran) 9 B1
Penllyn Avenue (Newport) 19 B2
Penllyn Lane.....................19 B2
Penllyn Lane.....................19 B2
Penmaes Road 7 D3
Penney Crescent................13 C2
Pennyfarthing Lane 27 C4
Pennyfields........................7 D5
Penrhos Villas..................15 A3
Penrice Green (8)..............10 E4
Pensarn Way......................8 G3
Pensidan View...................17 C2
Penterry Park 31 C2
Pentonville.......................14 H3
Pentovey Place 6 H5
Pentre Close 8 G4
Pentre Lane 11 A4/13 B1
Pentre Tai Lane....12 H1/17 A1
Pentre Tai Road..................17 B1
Pentrepoeth Close 17 D2
Pentrepoeth Road 17 D1
Pentrepoid Road........3 C2/D3
Pentwyn Close 32 E1
Pentwyn Heights 3 B2
Pentwyn Lane (Abersychan)
..................................3 B2
Pentwyn Lane (Newport) ..13 D1
Pentwyn Pitch*, Pentwyn Lane
..................................13 D1
Pentwyn Road 3 B2/C2
Pentwyn Terrace (Abersychan)
..................................3 B2
Pentwyn Terrace (Marshfield)
..................................30 H3
Pentwyn Villas*, Pentwyn Road
..................................3 B2
Penwern Cottages...............5 A6
Penycae Road 2 H2
Penygarn Road 3 D5
Penygraig Terrace 4 G6
Penygroes Cottages 17 D1
Penylan Close (Newport)...17 C3
Penylan Close (Pontypool) .5 D5
Penylan Cottages 18 F1
Penylan Court*, Penylan Road
..................................8 F4
Penylan Fields 2 F2
Penylan Road (Cwmbran)...8 F4
Penylan Road (Newport)...16 H3
Penylan Road (Varteg) ..2 F2/G1
Penylan Way......................8 G4
Penyrheol Road 4 H5
Penywain Cottages*,
    Penywain Road 4 E4
Penywain Lane..................4 F4
Penywain Road..................4 F4
Penywain Street.................4 E4

Pen Bedw.........................9 C4
Pen Mynydd Close 1 B5
Pen y Bryn 4 E6/5 A1
Pen y Bryn Close 13 D1
Pen y Cae Cottages 30 F2
Pen y Groes Grove 17 C2
Pen y Lan Road 17 D3
Pen y Llan Lane 5 C6
Pen y Parc 9 A1
Penarth Court 10 F4
Pencarn Avenue 18 G6
Pencarn Lane........18 G6/20 G1
Pencarn Way 18 F6/20 G1
Pencoed Place 9 A3
Penda Place....................31 D6
Penywain Terrace 4 E4
Penywaun Close*,
    Penywaun Road 8 E6
Penywaun Road 8 E5/E6/F5
Pepys Grove 19 D1
Percy Street 2 G1
Peregrine Court 27 B5
Perry Court 7 C4
Perthy Close 8 G5
Pettingale Road 9 B4
Phillip Street (Blaenavon) ...1 B4
Phillip Street (Newport) 21 A1
Phillips Green (9).............17 A4
Phillsay House 8 G5
Phoenix Drive 32 F5
Piccadilly Lane..................31 A1
Pickett Lane 22 F4
Picton Road 3 A2
Picton Street 6 E2
Picton Walk 8 E5
Picwic Green 8 E4
Piercefield Avenue 31 B2
Piercefield Cottages (2)....31 B1
Pike Cottages 25 C3
Pike Road 25 C2/C3
Pill Road 29 C1
Pill Row 29 C1
Pill Way 29 C1
Pill, The...........................29 C1
Pillmawr Circle.................13 D4
Pillmawr Court*, Pilton Vale
..................................13 D4
Pillmawr Road (Caerleon).15 D1
Pillmawr Road (Newport)
..............................13 D4/D5
Pilton Vale.................13 D4/D5
Pine Gardens.....................4 F3
Pine Grove 20 F2
Pine Tree Road 5 D4
Pinewood Close 13 D4
Pinnell Place 19 C5
Piper Close 16 F3
Pisgah Close 2 H1
Pisgah Hill 2 H1
Pisgah Road......................2 H1
Place de Cormeilles 31 C3
Plane Tree Close 15 D2
Plantation Drive 9 C4
Plantation, The..................27 C4
Plas Bryn Gomer...............9 A3
Plas Cwrt 10 G3
Plas Derwen 9 C4
Plas Ebbw 9 C2
Plas Geler Cottages*, Greenway
..................................2 H1
Plas Graig.........................9 C2
Plas Islwyn 9 C1
Plas Mawr 30 G5
Plas Trosant 9 C2
Plas Twyn 12 G1
Plas Ty Coch 10 G2
Plasycoed Road 4 F1
Playford Crescent.............23 C2
Pleasant Court 3 B3
Pleasant View (5) (Pontypool)
..................................3 D3
Pleasant View (Talywain)...3 A2
Plough Road 5 B5
Plover Close 21 D6
Plover Crescent 28 G6
Plum Tree Lane 28 G4
Plym Walk 13 D1
Pollard Close.....................9 C2
Pont Faen Road 21 C5
Pont y Felin Avenue 6 E3

Pont y Felin Lane...............6 F4
Pont y Felin Road...............6 E3
Pontaphywell 4 F5
Ponthir Road.....................15 A3
Pontnewydd Walk...............9 C2
Pontrhydyrun House...........9 A3
Pontrhydyrun Road 9 A2
Pontycraig Cottages...........12 E1
Pontymason Close 12 G2
Pontymason Court 12 G2
Pontymason Lane 12 E1
Pontymason Row 12 G2
Pontymoel Turnpike 5 C2
Pontypool Bypass (West)...4 E4
Pontypool Road 30 F4
Pool Lane 16 G1
Poplar Avenue....................5 D4
Poplar Close....................28 G2
Poplar Court 15 C2
Poplar Road (Cwmbran) 9 C3
Poplar Road (Newport) 21 A4
Poplar Terrace (7) 3 D3
Poplars, The.....................31 B4
Poppy Place 12 G1
Port Road 19 D4
Porthmawr Road 9 C1
Porthmawr Road Bungalows
..................................9 C2
Porthycarne Close 30 F5
Porthycarne Gate 30 F4
Porthycarne Street............30 F5
Portland Street 19 C6
Portskewett Street 21 B2
Portwall Road 31 C4
Post Gwynne 30 H2
Post Office Row 29 D4
Post Office Terrace 15 B6
Postern (20) 8 F5
Potter Street 19 C6
Potters Croft 32 G6
Potters Parade 19 C6
Pottery Road 19 D6
Pottery Terrace 19 D5
Pound Hill 18 F1
Pound Lane 26 G2
Powells Place 19 B6
Power Street 14 G4
Powis Almshouses*, Bridge St.
..................................31 B4
Prescoch Lane.......4 H6/5 D1
Presteigne Walk 8 F5
Preston Avenue 19 B2
Preston Close 32 G5
Price Avenue 3 C5
Price Close (Newport) 19 C5
Price Close (Pontypool) 3 C5
Priestley Close 19 D2
Primrose Cottages 4 F3
Primrose Court 8 F3
Primrose Way 12 G1
Prince Street (Blaenavon) ...1 C4
Prince Street (Newport) 14 H6
Prince Street (Pontypool) ...4 F4
Princes Walk 5 D5
Priory Close (Caerleon).....15 D1
Priory Close (Caldicot)......27 C4
Priory Close (Chepstow) ...31 B2
Priory Court (Magor) 27 C4
Priory Court (Usk) 30 G5
Priory Crescent*, Priory Way
..................................23 A3
Priory Drive 23 A3
Priory Gardens (Usk) 30 G5
Priory Gardens*, Priory Way
..................................23 A3

Priory Grove*, Priory Way.23 A3
Priory Street 30 G5
Priory Way 23 A3
Priory, The....................31 C4
Probert Place..................21 A1
Proposed M4 Relief Road
............18 H1/20 H3/22 F2
Prospect Cottages...........31 A5
Prospect Crescent 28 G6
Prospect Place (Abersychan)
...............................3 A2
Prospect Place (Cwmbran)
.................................10 E1
Prospect Place (Pontnewynydd)
..................................3 D2
Prospect Place (Pontypool).6 E4
Prospect Place (Varteg) 2 E1
Prospect Street 14 G4
Prossers Houses 4 F3
Pugsley Street................14 H5
Pump Street...................19 A4
Purcell Square................21 A5
Pwllmeyric Close.............32 E1
Pye Corner 17 C5
Q
Quantock Drive 16 H5
Quarry Cottages (Pontypool)
...................................4 E6
Quarry Cottages (Undy) ...27 B4
Quarry Rise 27 B4
Quarry Road......................4 H5
Quebec Close.................17 B6
Queen Street (Blaenavon) ..1 B4
Queen Street (Griffithstown)6 E2
Queen Street (Newport) 19 B5
Queen Street (Pontypool)....4 F4
Queen Victoria Almshouses*,
Stow Hill 19 B3
Queens Close 14 H4
Queens Croft..................14 H4
Queens Gardens 27 B3
Queens Hill 14 H4
Queens Hill Crescent 14 H4
Queens Road 32 E3
Queens Way 21 D6
Queensway 19 A4
Queensway Meadows.21 C4/D6
Quilter Close 21 B6
R
Race Road 4 G4
Rachel Square 20 G2
Radnor Road..................16 G1
Radnor Way 10 E2
Raglan Close 3 A2
Raglan Court (Cwmbran) ...9 A2
Raglan Court (Newport) 19 C5
Raglan Mews 20 H1
Raglan Way 32 F4
Railway Cottages (Abersychan)
...................................3 A3
Railway Cottages (Pontypool)
...................................6 G3
Railway Parade (10)...........3 D3
Railway Street (Caerleon).15 D4
Railway Street (Newport)..19 A4
Railway Terrace (Blaenavon)
...................................1 C3
Railway Terrace (Caerleon)
.................................15 D4
Railway Terrace (Pontypool)
...................................6 G2
Railway View..................28 G6
Ramp Cottages 27 C5
Ramp, The......................27 C5

Ramsey Walk (Cwmbran) ...7 B5
Ramsey Walk Close 16 G2
Ramsey Walk*,
Ramsey Walk Cl. 16 G2
Ramsey Walk*,................16 G2
Rankine Close 13 D2
Rannock House..................8 E5
Raphael Close 16 G2
Ravenscourt 7 D4
Rector Road 25 B4
Rectory Gardens 27 C6
Red Hill........................30 G6
Red House Road 26 F5
Red Lion Flats*, Foundry Road
...................................3 B2
Redbrook House*,
Redbrook Way 9 D2
Redbrook Road 19 A1
Redbrook Way 9 D2
Redd Landes 26 F5
Reddings, The 32 F4
Rede Road........................8 F5
Redland Street 14 G4
Redlands, The 21 B5
Redmeadow Crescent*,
Moorlands View 28 G6
Redvers Street 21 B2
Redwick Court 10 E2
Redwick House*, Redwick Ct.
.................................10 E2
Redwood Close (Caerleon)
.................................15 D1
Redwood Close (Chepstow)
.................................32 F3
Reene Court 21 B3
Rees Close 13 C3
Regent Way 31 C3
Reginald Terrace (10) 17 A4
Rembrandt Way..............16 F2
Renoir Road 16 G3
Reservoir Close 17 A5
Restway Wall..................31 C4
Reynolds Close 16 F2
Rhiw Melin......................7 A5
Rhodri Place (9) 10 E4
Rhuddlan Close 17 B2
Rhyd Tre Derwen 3 D2
Rhyd y Nos Street 1 B4
Rhymney Court 7 C4
Ribble Square 13 D1
Ribble Walk 13 D1
Richmond Close 9 B1
Richmond Place 9 B1
Richmond Road (Cwmbran)9 B1
Richmond Road (Newport)
.................................16 G1
Richmond Road (Pontypool)
...................................6 G2
Richmond Street................9 B1
Ridgeway (Newport).........19 B1
Ridgeway (Pontypool).......3 D6
Ridgeway Avenue 19 A1
Ridgeway Close 19 A2
Ridgeway Court 19 A2
Ridgeway Crescent 19 A1
Ridgeway Drive 19 A2
Ridgeway Grove..............19 A1
Ridgeway Hill.................19 A2
Ridgeway Park Road 19 A2

Ringwood Avenue 16 H5
Ringwood Hill 16 H5
Ringwood Place*, Ringwood Hill
.................................16 H5
Risca Road (Newport) .19 B1/B2
Risca Road (Rogerstone)..12 F1
Rise, The..........................7 B6
Rising Sun Gardens 15 C3
River Row (17)...................3 D3
River View (Chepstow) ...31 C4
River View (Newport).......16 F1
Rivermead Way 12 G1
Riverside (Caerleon) 15 B3
Riverside (Garndiffaith)......2 H2
Riverside (Newport) 14 H6
Riverside (Pontypool)........4 E5
Riverside Cottages*, School La.
...................................3 A3
Riverside Court 4 F5
Riverside Drive 1 C4
Riverside Estate.......15 A2/B6
Riverside Mill 31 B5
Riverside*, The Back.......31 B4
Riversmead 10 E3
Riverview*, The Moorings .16 F2
Roath Court 9 D3
Robbins Lane 19 B5
Robert Place 19 C5
Roberts Close 13 C3
Robertson Way 13 C3
Rochdale Terrace (1) 3 D3
Rochester Road 21 A2
Rock Cottages 28 E4
Rock Lodge 25 D2
Rock Villa Close 2 F1
Rock Villa Lane 31 B5
Rockfield Close 24 F6
Rockfield Crescent 27 B6
Rockfield Glade 24 F6
Rockfield Grove 27 B6
Rockfield Houses 4 E5
Rockfield Rise.................27 B5
Rockfield Street...............14 G6
Rockfield Way 27 B6
Rockhill Road 4 G6/5 C1
Rockwood Cottages.........31 D4
Rockwood Road 31 D3
Roding Close 12 E6
Rodney Parade 19 A5
Rodney Road.........14 H5/19 A6
Rogiet Road 28 G2
Rogiet Terrace 28 G1
Roland Villas*, Freeholdland Rd.
...................................3 C3
Rolls Close 8 E4
Rolls Walk 12 H4
Roman Gates 15 D4
Roman Reach 15 D1
Roman Road 24 G1
Roman Way...........15 C2/C3
Romney Close 16 G3
Romsley Court..................8 E6
Ronald Road 16 G1
Rosamund Close..............20 H2
Rose Cottages (Chepstow)
.................................32 G1
Rose Cottages (Garndiffaith)
...................................2 H2
Rose Cottages (Talywain)...2 H1
Rose Cottages (Upper Race)
...................................4 H4
Rose Cottages (Varteg) 2 E3
Rose Court 8 E3
Rose Garden, The (Newport)
.................................19 A3

Rose Gardens (Cwmbran) ..9 C4
Rose Street 14 H4
Rose Terrace (6) 3 D2
Rose Villas*, Manor Road ...3 A2
Rose Walk 12 G1
Rosebery Street 6 E2
Rosecroft Drive...............23 A4
Rosemary Cottages*,
Freeholdland Road ...3 C3
Rosemary Lane 4 F5
Rosemead 7 D3
Rosendale Court 16 H2
Ross House*, Victoria St...10 E1
Ross Lane 14 G4
Ross Street 14 F4
Rosser Street.....................4 E4
Rosslyn Road 21 A2
Rother Close 11 D6
Rothesay Road................21 A2
Rougemont Grove 32 G5
Round Stables 3 B1
Roundwood Close............25 C1
Routes View 23 C4
Row, The (3) (St. Arvans) .31 B1
Row, The (Shirenewton)...26 F5
Rowan Close 27 B5
Rowan Court.....................8 F4
Rowan Crescent 6 F1/G2
Rowan Drive 32 F3
Rowan Way 13 C4
Rowland Villas..................3 C3
Royal Oak Drive 16 G6/23 B1
Royal Oak Green 9 C4
Royal Oak Hill 16 F6
Royce Walk 12 H4
Royston Crescent 21 B4
Rubens Close 16 G2
Rudry Street...................14 H6
Ruffetts Close 31 C2
Rugby Road 19 A6
Rumney Walk (10)............10 E4
Ruperra Close 17 C4
Ruperra Lane 19 B5
Ruperra Street.................19 B5
Rupert Brooke Drive.........19 C2
Rush Wall 27 D2
Rushbrook 7 D4
Ruskin Avenue 12 G3/G4
Ruskin Close 8 E4
Ruskin Rise 19 D1
Russell Close (Newport) ...17 B3
Russell Close (Pontypool)...5 D5
Russell Drive 13 D3
Russell Drive Gardens 13 D3
Russell House*, Richmond St.
...................................9 B1
Russell Street 9 B1
Russet Close 23 A4
Ruth Road 5 C3
Rutherford Hill 13 D3
Rutland Place 19 C5
S
Saffron Court 8 F3
Salisbury Close (Newport) ...3 B3
Salisbury Court 7 D6
Salisbury Terrace 2 E2
Samsons Avenue 12 F2
Sandpiper Way 20 G1
Sandy Lane (Caerwent) 26 H3
Sandy Lane (Caldicot).......28 E4
Sandy Lane (Castleton).....30 F1
Sandy Lane (Newport) 20 E2
Sandybrook Close 8 F6
Sawtells Terrace (7) 3 D2
Saxon Place 31 D6

Saxons Houses 3 A2
Scarborough Road 16 F1
Scard Street.....................19 A4
School Close 4 G4
School Cottages (Mathern)
.................................32 G1
School Cottages*, Tump Lane
.................................27 C5
School Court...................10 E1
School Crescent 6 G2
School Hill 31 C4
School Houses*, Bailey St.19 A4
School Lane (Abersychan)...3 A3
School Lane (Garndiffaith)..2 G2
School Lane (Newport) 19 A5
School Lane (Pontypool).....4 E4
School Park 27 B4
School Road (Abersychan) .3 B2
School Road (Cwmbran).....7 A5
School Road (Penperlleni) ..5 B6
School Road (Pontypool) ...3 D3
School Terrace (12)
(Pontnewynydd) 3 D2
School Terrace (Rogerstone)
.................................17 A2
School View............4 G6/5 C1
Scott Close 19 D1
Scott Walk 12 G4
Sea Street Lane 27 D1
Sea View 29 D3
Sea View Terrace.............28 H1
Seasons Close 27 B3
Seaview Terrace 19 B4
Second Street..................22 E3
Sedbury Lane 31 B5/B6/C6
Sedgemoor Court.............14 G3
Selby Close 10 E4
Serpentine Road 19 A4
Seven Stiles Avenue 21 C6
Severn Avenue 31 B5
Severn Bridge Park Homes
.................................32 F6
Severn Bridge, The (M48).32 H5
Severn Crescent 31 D4
Severn Terrace................19 B4
Severn View (Caldicot).....28 G4
Severn View (Chepstow) .31 C3
Severn View (Cwmbran) 7 A4
Severn View (Garndiffaith)..2 G2
Severn View Terrace..........3 B2
Sevins (21)........................8 F5
Seymour Avenue 24 E6
Seymour Rise..................24 E6
Shaftesbury Court (4).......14 H4
Shaftesbury Street (5)......14 H5
Shaftesbury Walk (6)........14 H5
Shakespeare Close 28 G3
Shakespeare Crescent19 C1/D1
Shakespeare Drive 28 G3
Shakespeare Road..............8 E6
Shakespeare Row*,
Shakespeare Drive ..28 G3
Shannon Close.................13 D2
Sharps Way (3)................32 F5
Shaw Grove 19 D1
Shawley Court 8 E6
Shea Gardens*, Francis Drive
.................................19 C5
Sheaf Lane 14 H6
Shelley Close 28 G3
Shelley Green....................8 E6
Shelley Road 21 A4
Shepherd Drive 24 H2
Shepherds Hill Caravan Site
...................................4 H4

Sherbourne Court 6 G2
Sherbourne Road.................6 G2
Sheridan Close.....................19 D1
Shetland Close....................16 G2
Shetland Walk.....................16 G2
Shires, The.........................30 G2
Shop Road..........................2 E2
Shop Row............................27 D1
Short Path (22).....................8 F5
Shrewsbury Close (7).......14 H5
Sickert Close.......................16 G3
Sid Griffiths Court...............2 H2
Sidney Street......................19 A4
Silleys Close........................31 A5
Silver Birch Close..............15 D1
Silver Fir Square.................17 B5
Simpson Close....................13 C3
Sims Square........................21 A5
Sir Charles Crescent.........20 G2
Sir Charles Square.............20 G2
Sirhowy Court.....................7 C4
Siskin Crescent*, Barn Owl Rd.
...............................28 G1
Sixth Street.........................22 F3
Skinner Row........................21 B5
Skinner Street.....................19 A5
Slade Street........................21 B2
Slade View..........................28 G1
Slate Houses......................3 D2
Slate Row............................2 E2
Slipway Cottages...............22 F2
Sluvad Lane.........................6 E6
Sluvad Road........................6 E5
Smallbrook Close...............10 E2
Smithfield Cottages...........18 G4
Snail Creep..........................2 E2
Snail Creep Terrace...........2 E3
Snatchwood Court..............3 C3
Snatchwood Road...............3 C3
Snatchwood Terrace..........3 B2
Sneyd Park*, Malpas Rd...13 C3
Snowdon Court....................9 B3
Soane Close........................12 G4
Soar Close...........................9 B4
Soho Street.....................21 A1/A2
Somerset Cottages...........31 B4
Somerset Road (Cwmbran) 9 C2
Somerset Road (Newport) 16 G1
Somerset Way.....................32 F4
Somerton Court...................21 C3
Somerton Crescent............21 A4
Somerton Lane....................21 B3
Somerton Park....................21 B3
Somerton Place*, Chepstow Rd.
...............................21 A2
Somerton Road............21 A3/B3
Sorrel Drive.........................14 H3
South Avenue......................6 G1
South Close 10 F4
South Court (16)..................3 D3
South Grove........................28 G1
South Market Street 19 B6
South Road..........................10 G2
South Row...........................27 D1
South Street........................6 G2
South View (Chepstow)....31 B5
South View (Llanvaches) ..25 B3
South View (Pontnewynydd)
...............................3 C3
South View (Pontypool).....4 F4
South View Terrace (8).......1 C4
South Walk..........................9 D1
Southbrook View................29 C2
Southern Distributor Road
...............................18 H4

Southville Road 19 A3
Sovereign Arcade*, Kingsway
...............................19 B5
Spartan Close......................23 A4
Speke Street........................21 A1
Spencer Road......................19 B3
Spinney, The 13 D4
Spouts Hill...........................26 F6
Spring Grove 7 D3
Spring Lane.........................9 C3
Spring Street........................14 F4
Spring Terrace.....................6 F1
Springfield Close (Cwmbran)
...............................9 A3
Springfield Close (Newport)
...............................17 B1
Springfield Court.................23 D5
Springfield Drive................16 H6
Springfield Houses (8).......3 D2
Springfield Lane..................17 B1
Springfield Road (Newport)
...............................17 B1
Springfield Road (Pontypool)
...............................6 G1
Springfield Terrace (New Inn)
...............................6 E4
Springfield Terrace
(Plas-y-coed)...4 E1
Springfield Villas*, Wainfelin Rd.
...............................4 E4
Springfields........................30 F2
Springvale..................7 C5/D5
Spytty Lane........................21 C3
Spytty Road...................21 C3/C5
Square, The (Abersychan)..3 B3
Square, The (Cwmbran).....7 A3
Square, The (Magor)...........27 C3
Squires Close.....................12 H4
Squires Gate.......................12 H4
Squirrel Cottages...............31 B1
St. Andrews Avenue...........31 D4
St. Andrews Close..............9 A2
St. Ann Street.....................31 B4
St. Annes Close (Cwmbran)9 B1
St. Annes Close (Newport)17 A5
St. Annes Crescent (Newport)
...............................16 G1
St. Annes Crescent (Undy)
...............................27 C6
St. Anthonys Close 6 F1
St. Arvans Court.................31 B1
St. Arvans Road..................9 D2
St. Augustine Road.............6 F1
St. Basils Crescent............17 C4
St. Basils Stores.................17 C4
St. Benedict Close..............6 F1
St. Benedict Court..............17 C4
St. Briavels House*, Oaksford
...............................8 E3
St. Briavels Mews...............20 H1
St. Brides Close (Cwmbran)
...............................10 E4
St. Brides Close (Magor)...27 B3
St. Brides Crescent............20 E2
St. Brides Gardens.............20 E2
St. Brides Road..................27 A3
St. Cadocs Close...............15 C3
St. Cadocs Road.................3 D6
St. Cecilia Court*, Gold Tops
...............................19 A4
St. Cybi Avenue..................24 F1
St. Cybi Drive......................24 F1
St. Cybi Rise.......................24 F1
St. Davids Close (Chepstow)
...............................31 D4

St. Davids Close (Pontypool)
...............................4 E6
St. Davids Court (Magor) ..27 C3
St. Davids Court (Marshfield)
...............................30 H3
St. Davids Crescent 19 D2
St. Davids Road.................9 C2
St. Dials Court*, St. Dials Road
...............................7 D6
St. Dials Road....................7 D5/D6
St. Dominics Retreat.........4 G4
St. Donats Close (11).......10 E4
St. Dubricius Gardens......27 C6
St. Edward Street...............19 B4
St. Ewens Road.................32 E4
St. George Road................31 D4
St. Georges Crescent.......16 G2
St. Georges Way 32 F6
St. Hildas Road..................6 F2
St. James Field..................4 F5
St. Johns Close 4 E3
St. Johns Court (Rogerstone)
...............................12 H2
St. Johns Court*, Oakfield Rd.
...............................19 A3
St. Johns Crescent (Newport)
...............................12 H2
St. Johns Crescent (Pontypool)
...............................4 E3
St. Johns Gardens.............31 C2
St. Johns Road...................16 H2
St. Joseph Place...............10 H4
St. Josephs Close..............27 C6
St. Julians Avenue.............16 G1
St. Julians Court.................16 G1
St. Julians Park*, Stockton Rd.
...............................14 F6
St. Julians Road.................16 G1
St. Julians Street...............19 B4
St. Kingsmark Avenue........31 B2
St. Lawrence Lane..............31 D1
St. Lawrence Road.............31 B2
St. Lukes Close..................3 A2
St. Lukes Road...................6 E1
St. Marks Crescent............14 H4
St. Martins Court*, Gaer Road
...............................19 C2/C3
St. Mary Court 19 A4
St. Mary Street...................19 A4
St. Mary Street (Chepstow)
...............................31 C4
St. Marys Close..................6 E1
St. Marys Crescent 28 G1
St. Marys Place..................29 C2
St. Marys Road (Cwmbran) 9 C3
St. Marys Road (Nash) 22 H5
St. Marys Street (Pontypool)
...............................6 E1
St. Marys Way....................30 G5
St. Matthews Road....4 G6/5 C1
St. Maur Gardens...............31 B3
St. Maur House*,
    St. Maur Gardens....31 B3
St. Mellons Close...............27 B5
St. Mellons Road................30 H2
St. Michael Grove..............10 H4
St. Michael Street..............19 C6
St. Oswalds Close..............6 G2
St. Peters Close*, Ty Gwyn Rd.
...............................8 F4
St. Phillips Flats*, Cromwell Rd.
...............................21 B2
St. Stephens Close 26 G3
St. Stephens Court............27 C6
St. Stephens Place............27 B6

St. Stephens Road.............19 D6
St. Tathans Place...............26 G3
St. Tecla Road....................32 E3
St. Teilo Court....................27 C6
St. Tewdric Road................31 D3
St. Tewdrics Place.............32 G1
St. Thomas Court 3 A1
St. Vincent Lane.................14 H6
St. Vincent Road................14 H5
St. Woolos Court................19 B4
St. Woolos Green...............9 C2
St. Woolos Place................19 B4
St. Woolos Road................19 B4
Stable Row 1 B3
Stafford Road (Caldicot) ...28 G5
Stafford Road (Newport)...14 G6
Stafford Road (Pontypool) ..5 D1
Stamford Court...................14 H4
Stanford Road....................21 A6
Stanley Place.....................9 C1
Stanley Road (Garndiffaith)
...............................2 G2
Stanley Road (Newport)....19 A4
Star Lane............................3 D5
Star Road 5 B6
Star Street..........................10 E1
Star Villas...........................15 A3
Starling Close*, Barn Owl Road
...............................28 G1
Station Approach (Caerleon)
...............................15 D4
Station Approach (Newport)
...............................17 C4
Station Bungalows..............29 B4
Station Close*, Station Road
...............................28 G1
Station Cottages.................10 F4
Station Farm.......................9 C3
Station Houses...................2 E3
Station Road (Caerleon) ...15 D4
Station Road (Caldicot).....28 H4
Station Road (Chepstow)..31 C4
Station Road (Cwmbran)....9 B1
Station Road (Llanwern) ...23 D3
Station Road (Ponthir) .15 A1/B5
Station Road (Pontypool) ...6 E2
Station Road (Portskewett)
...............................29 B4
Station Road (Rogiet).........28 G1
Station Street (Abersychan) 3 B3
Station Street (Newport).....19 A4
Station Terrace (Blaenavon)
...............................1 C4
Station Terrace (Cwmbran).9 B1
Steep Street.......................31 C3
Steepfield...........................9 B3
Steer Crescent...................16 G3
Stelvio Park Avenue...........19 B2
Stelvio Park Court 19 B3
Stelvio Park Crescent........19 B2
Stelvio Park Drive...............19 B2
Stephen Walk*, Cefn Wood
...............................17 A4
Stephenson Street...19 D6/22 E1
Stepping Stones.................5 A5
Sterndale Bennett Road....23 C1
Stevelee.............................8 F5
Stevenson Close................12 H4
Stevenson Court................12 H4
Steynton Path....................8 E5
Stiels..................................8 G5
Stockton Close...................16 E1
Stockton Road....................14 F6
Stokes Court......................15 A2/B6
Stokes Drive.......................15 A2/B6

Stone Cottages 29 D4
Stoney Road.......................2 H2
Stour Court.........................7 C4
Stow Hill..................19 B3/B4/B5
Stow Park Avenue..............19 B4
Stow Park Circle.................19 B3
Stow Park Court*, Stow Hill
...............................19 B4
Stow Park Crescent...........19 B3
Stow Park Drive..................19 B3
Stow Park Gardens............19 B3
Stowe Path (12)..................10 E4
Strand, The.........................9 D1
Striguil Road.......................32 E3
Strongbow Road 31 D4
Stuart Avenue.....................31 B2
Sudbrook Road...................29 C3
Sudbury Walk*, Evans St...14 G5
Sullivan Circle....................21 A6
Summerhill Avenue............16 H1
Summerhill Court (7)...........2 G1
Summerhouse Lane............32 F5
Sunlea Crescent.................5 B3
Sunny Bank (Blaenavon) ...1 A3
Sunny Bank (Garndiffaith)...2 H2
Sunny Place.......................15 A5
Sunnybank (Cwmbran).......8 G2
Sunnybank (Newport) 17 C2
Sunnybank Court................6 E2
Sunnybank Road................6 E1
Sunnybank Way..................6 F1
Sunnyside (Penperlleni) ...5 A6
Sunnyside (Usk).................30 F6
Surrey Place......................16 G1
Sussex Close.....................21 C3
Sutherland Crescent 16 G3
Sutton Road.......................14 G6
Swallow Drive....................28 G5
Swallow Way 20 F1
Swan Close.........................28 G5
Swan Square......................3 A2
Sward Close.......................12 G4
Swinburne Close.................16 H3
Sycamore Avenue (Caldicot)
...............................28 F4
Sycamore Avenue (Chepstow)
...............................32 F3
Sycamore Avenue (Newport)
...............................21 A3
Sycamore Court (Chepstow)
...............................31 B1
Sycamore Court (Cwmbran)
...............................8 G2
Sycamore Place.................7 B5
Sycamore Road..................6 F1
Sycamore Road South.......6 G1
Sycamore Terrace..............27 C4
Sycamores, The*, Albion Road
...............................4 G4
Sychan Terrace..................3 B2
Sylvan Close.......................13 C4
Symondscliff Way...............29 C1
T
Tabernacle Road................25 B3
Taff Court............................7 B4
Taff Road.....................28 E5/F5
Talbot Lane.........................19 A5
Talfan Close 3 C5
Talgarth Close....................10 E2
Taliesin 9 C1
Taliesin Close.....................12 H4
Taliesin Drive.....................12 H4
Tallards Place.....................31 C6
Tallis Close.........................23 D1

Talywain House*, Woodlands
....2 H1
Tamar Close...............14 E2
Tan House Court..............26 G3
Tan House Drive..........16 E5
Tan y Coed.....................3 D3
Tatton Road....................22 E6
Teal Close....................27 B5
Tees Close................13 D2
Tegfan Court...................8 G3
Telford Close..............12 H4
Telford Street................21 A1
Tempest Drive.............31 C2
Temple Street..............19 C6
Tenby Close...................9 D4
Tenison Road...................3 D6
Tennyson Avenue*, Station Rd.
....23 D3
Tennyson Close..........28 G3
Tennyson Road (Newport)
....21 A2
Tennyson Road (Caldicot)28 G3
Tern Court.......................7 C4
Terrace, The...............29 C3
Terry Morgan Bungalows....1 C5
Tetbury Close...............14 G5
Tewdrick Court................9 C4
Tewends (23)..................8 F5
Tewkesbury Walk (8)......14 H5
Teynes............................8 F5
Thames Close..............14 E1
Third Street..................22 E3
Thirlmere Place..............16 F1
Thistle Court...................8 E3
Thomas Grove..............17 A4
Thomas Street..............31 C3
Thompson Avenue........21 B4
Thompson Close..........21 B4
Thorn Tree Drive (5).....32 F5
Thornbury Park...........17 A4/B4
Thornbury Park Lane 17 A4
Thorncliffe Court............8 E5
Thornhill Close...............7 A4
Thornhill Gardens.........12 G2
Thornhill Road...................7 C5
Thornhill Way..............12 G2
Thornwell Road.......32 E4/F4
Till Grove.....................15 C1
Tillsland........................8 G5
Tintern Close................10 E2
Tippet Close................23 C1
Tirpentwys Terrace......4 E2
Tolpath...........................8 F3
Tom Mann Close........16 G6
Ton Bach Street.............1 C4
Ton Mawr Avenue.........1 C4
Ton Mawr Road..............1 C4
Ton Mawr Street.............1 C4
Ton Road (Cwmbran)....8 E4/F5
Ton Road (Llangybi).....24 F1
Ton Road Cottages.......24 F1
Tone Close...................11 D6
Tone Road...................11 D6
Tone Square................11 D6
Top Road........................2 G2
Torfaen Terrace (19).......3 D3
Toronto Close...............17 B6
Torridge Road.............11 D6
Tower Court*, London St. .16 H1
Towers, The....................9 D2
Tram Cottages............10 H5
Tram Lane....................10 H6
Tram Road (Caerleon) 15 D4
Tram Road (Cwmbran) 7 A4
Tramway Close...............8 F3

Tranch Road.................4 F3
Trannon Court................7 C4
Tranquil Place.............10 F1
Tranters Terrace.............7 A5
Traston Avenue...........21 D4
Traston Close...............21 D4
Traston Lane................21 D4
Traston Road................22 E2
Traws Mawr Cottages....13 B1
Traws Mawr Lane.........13 C1
Treberth Estate......16 H6/23 B1
Tredegar Court.............19 D5
Tredegar Drive.............27 B5
Tredegar House Drive 20 G1
Tredegar Park View......17 B5
Tredegar Street (Newport) 19 B6
Tredegar Street (Rhiwderin)
....17 B1
Trees Close.................13 D2
Tregare Street..............14 H6
Tregarn Close...............24 G2
Tregarn Court...............24 G2
Tregarn Road................24 H1
Tregwilym Close...........17 B4
Tregwilym Road....17 A2/A4/B3
Tregwilym Walk*, Tregwilym Rd.
....17 B4
Treherbert Road.............9 A4
Trelawny Close.............30 F6
Trellech Close...............10 E2
Trem Twyn Barlwm.......10 F1
Trem y Mynydd Court.......1 C5
Trent Road....................11 D6
Tretower Court (13).......10 E4
Trevine Path....................8 E5
Trevithick Close...........13 C2
Trinity Court.................19 C6
Trinity Lane..................15 D2
Trinity Place.................19 C6
Trinity Road 7 C6/9 B1
Trinity View.................15 D1
Troddi Close.................28 E5
Trosmawr Road*, St. Dials Rd.
....10 E1
Trosnant Street 4 G5/G6
Trosnant Villa.................4 G6
Trostrey.........................8 G5
Trostrey Close................5 D5
Trostrey Street.............14 H6
Trussel Road...................9 C2
Tubular Cottages..........31 B5
Tudor Court.................27 C5
Tudor Crescent 17 A4/A5
Tudor Drive..................31 C2
Tudor Road (Cwmbran) 9 D1
Tudor Road (Newport)....16 F1
Tudor Woods...............10 E4
Tump Lane...................27 C5
Tunnel Court................19 A4
Turberville Road.............9 C2
Turner Street................14 H6
Turners End (26)............8 F4
Turnpike Close (Chepstow)
....31 C2
Turnpike End...............32 F6
Turnpike Road.......9 D4/10 E4
Turnstiles, The..............14 G5
Tutshill Gardens...........31 B5
Tweedy Lane................21 A2
Twin Cottages.......15 A3/B6
Twinings, The.................8 E4
Twisells Road.................4 F3
Twm Barlwm View......10 E4

Twmbarlwm Rise...........8 F2
Twmpath Gardens.........4 G4
Twmpath Road..............4 F4
Two Locks Road 8 F6/10 F1
Twyn Oaks...................15 C5
Twyn Square...............30 G5
Ty Box Close..................9 B1
Ty Box Cottages............9 C1
Ty Box Road...................9 C1
Ty Brith Gardens..........30 G5
Ty Canol Court...............8 F3
Ty Canol Row.................8 F3
Ty Canol Way..................8 E3
Ty Coch Close..............17 C3
Ty Coch Lane ...10 G1/H2/13 A2
Ty Coch Way.................10 F1
Ty Draw.........................6 G6
Ty Draw Lane.................6 G6
Ty Dwmpyn Road...........4 E1
Ty Fry............................1 B4
Ty Fry Close...................1 B4
Ty Gwyn Road (Cwmbran)
...............................7 D5/8 E3
Ty Gwyn Road (Little Mill)...6 G6
Ty Gwyn Road (Varteg).....2 F2
Ty Gwyn Way.................7 D4
Ty Mawr Lane..............30 H3
Ty Mynydd......................9 C2
Ty Mynydd Close............1 B5
Ty Pwca Place................7 A5
Ty Pwca Road................7 A5
Ty Rosser Gwyn.............2 G2
Ty Trappa Place..............7 B6
Ty Trappa Road..............7 B6
Ty Tudor..........................9 D2
Tydies............................8 G5
Tydu View....................17 A5
Tylers Way...................31 C6
Tyllwyd Road...............19 A3
Tyn y Nant Cottages......18 H1
Tyne Close...................12 E6
Tynewydd Avenue..........9 B1
Tynewydd Court.............9 B1
Tynewydd Drive...........30 F1
Tynewydd Farm Close.....9 A1
Tynewydd Green............9 B1
Tynewydd House*,
          Tynewydd Road.........9 B2
Tynewydd North Close.....9 A1
Tynewydd Road..............9 B2
Tynewydd South Close....9 B1
U
Ullswater Court..............7 D5
Union Street....................3 B2
Upland Drive...................3 C4
Uplands Court (Newport) ..16 H2
Uplands Court (Rogerstone)
....12 H3
Uplands Terrace.............7 D6
Uplands, The...............12 H3
Upper Brick Yard............1 A3
Upper Bridge Street........4 F5
Upper Church Street.....31 C4
Upper Coed Cae............1 B5
Upper Cwmbran Road 7 A4
Upper Dock Street........19 A5
Upper Five Houses..........2 E1
Upper Garn Terrace........1 A2
Upper Glantorvaen Terrace 1 C3
Upper Hill Street.............1 A3
Upper Nelson Street......31 C4
Upper Park Terrace........4 F5
Upper Power Street......14 G4
Upper Tennyson Road....16 H2
Upper Trosnant Street 4 G5

Upper Waun Street..........1 B3
Upper Woodland Street....1 B4
Upton Lane..................19 B2
Upton Road..................19 B2
Usk Bridge Mews..........30 G4
Usk Close....................28 E5
Usk Court.......................7 D4
Usk Road (Caerleon) 15 D4
Usk Road (Penperlleni) 5 B6
Usk Road (Pontypool)
...............................5 A4/B3/C3
Usk Road (Shirenewton)...26 E5
Usk Street...................14 G6
Usk Vale Close............15 D4
Usk Vale Drive.............15 D4
Usk Vale Mews............15 D4
Usk Vale View..............16 E5
Usk View......................16 F3
Usk Way..............19 A5/B6/D5
Ukside.........................15 D3
Uskside Cottages*, Ukside
....16 E5
Uskvale Court................5 B3
V
Vale View (Cwmbran) 8 G2
Vale View (Newport).....16 G3
Valentine Lane.............32 F5
Valentine Road...............3 B3
Van Dyke Close...........16 G2
Vanbrugh Close............12 H4
Vanbrugh Gardens.......19 D2
Vancouver Drive 17 B6/19 B1
Varteg Road............1 C4/2 F1
Varteg Waste.................2 F1
Varteg Waste House 2 F1
Vaughan Williams Drive ...21 A5
Vauxhall Lane..............31 C3
Vauxhall Road..............31 D3
Ventnor Road..............10 E2
Venture Park...............21 B1
Vermeer Crescent........16 G3
Vernon Grove...............26 H3
Veronica Close.............17 B5
Viaduct Court...........4 G6/5 C1
Viaduct Road.................2 H2
Viaduct Terrace.............2 H2
Viaduct View*, Viaduct Rd. .2 H2
Vicarage Close..............17 C4
Vicarage Gardens (Caerwent)
....26 G3
Vicarage Gardens (Marshfield)
....30 G2
Vicarage Gardens (Newport)
....12 G2
Vicarage Hill................19 B5
Vicarage Lane................2 H3
Vicarage Terrace............2 H3
Vicars Cottages*,
          Maesderwn Road....5 C1
Victoria Avenue...........16 H1
Victoria Close...............19 B5
Victoria Court...............16 H1
Victoria Crescent.........19 A4
Victoria Lane................16 H2
Victoria Mews*, Victoria Pl. 19 B5
Victoria Place (Abersychan) 2 H2
Victoria Place (Newport)...19 B5
Victoria Place*, Viaduct Rd. 2 H2
Victoria Road (Abersychan) 2 H2
Victoria Road (Chepstow) .32 F4
Victoria Road (Newport)...19 B5
Victoria Road (Pontypool)
...............................4 G6/5 C1
Victoria Street (Cwmbran) .10 E1
Victoria Street (Pontypool) .6 E2

Victoria Villas*, St. Lukes Road
....3 D3
Victoria Walk*, Commercial St.
....19 A5
Victoria Way...............27 B5
Villas, The...................29 C4
Vincent Street...............1 B4
Vine Cottages (3) (Caerleon)
....15 D4
Vine Cottages (Chepstow) 31 D3
Vine Place...................16 H1
Vinegar Hill.................27 A5
Violet Walk..................12 G1
Vivian Road.................21 A1
W
Wades, The (25)............8 F5
Waghausel Close.........28 G5
Wainfelin Avenue 4 E4
Wainfelin Road..............4 E4
Walden Grange Close....21 A4
Walford Davies Drive.....21 A5
Walford Street..............14 G4
Walk Farm Drive...........30 E1
Walk, The......................5 D4
Walkdens, The, (27).......8 F5
Walker Flats.................29 D4
Wallace Close...............30 F6
Wallis Street...............19 C6
Walmer Road...............21 A2
Walnut Drive...............15 D1
Walsall Street..............21 B1
Walton Close...............21 B5
Waltwood Park Drive.....23 C6
Waltwood Road............23 D5
Ward Close...................16 G3
Warlock Close..............23 C1
Warren Slade................32 F4
Warrendale (28)..............8 F4
Warwick Close (Chepstow)
....32 E3
Warwick Close (Cwmbran) .7 D3
Warwick Close (Pontypool) .6 F4
Warwick Lane*, Warwick Road
....21 A3
Warwick Road.............21 A3
Watchhouse Parade 19 D5
Waterloo Cottages.......10 F1
Waterloo Court..............6 G2
Waterloo Place..............3 A2
Waterloo Road (Newport) .19 C4
Waterloo Road (Talywain)...3 D2
Waters Lane................19 A5
Waters Road................31 D4
Waterside Close...........12 G2
Waterside Court (Newport)14 F5
Waterside Court*, Abbey Road
....10 E1
Waterside Walk West....12 H3
Waterworks Lane...........2 H3
Watkins Walk*, Cefn Wood
....17 A4
Watt Close (Newport).....13 C3
Watts Close (Rogerstone) .12 H5
Waun Allt y Rhyd............9 A3
Waun Blis......................9 A3
Waun Cottages............10 G6
Waun Hywel Road..........7 B6
Waun Road....................8 F6
Waun Wern....................4 G3
Waun Wern Caravan Park...4 G3
Waunddu.......................13 C3
Wavell Drive................13 C3
Waveney Close............11 D5
Waverley Terrace...4 G6/5 C1
Wayfield Crescent..........9 C1

Weare Close 11 D6
Webley Close 15 B3
Webley Gardens...............15 B3
Wedgwood Drive..............29 C3
Wednesbury Street...........21 B2
Weldon Close...................9 B4
Well Close (6) 32 F5
Well Cottages (Magor) 27 C1
Well Cottages (Portskewett)
....29 B3
Well Lane.........................25 A6
Welland Circle 11 D5
Welland Crescent 11 D5
Wellfield Court.................30 H2
Wellfield Lane..................6 G2
Wellfield Road 30 H2
Wellington Drive 7 D4
Wellington Lane................4 F3
Wellington Road (Newport)
....17 B6
Wellington Road (Talywain) 3 A1
Wells Close 19 D2
Wellwood Cottages (11).....3 D3
Welsh Street....................31 B2
Wentloog Close 9 D2
Wentsland Crescent 4 F3
Wentsland House*,
    Wentsland Road 4 G3
Wentsland Road 4 G3
Wentwood Close 7 B5
Wentwood Drive (Llanvaches)
....25 B3/B4
Wentwood Drive
    (Parc-Seymour)......24 E6
Wentwood Road...............15 D1
Wentwood View................28 E5
Wentworth Close 17 B2
Wern Fach Court...............8 G3
Wern Hill 4 F4
Wern Road........................6 G2
Wern School Close 6 G2
Wern Terrace (Newport) ...12 H3
Wern Terrace (Pontypool) ...4 F4
Wesley Close 10 E1
Wesley Place 19 A5
Wesley Street..................10 E1
Wesley Terrace 4 E1
West Avenue...................6 G1
West Bank.......................10 E4
West Bank Court (25)........3 D4
West End (Magor) 27 C3
West End (Undy)..............27 C5
West End Avenue 3 C3
West End Cottages (Caldicot)
....27 C5
West End Cottages (Magor)
....27 C3
West Hill Road.................3 C4
West Market Street...........19 B6
West Nash Road...............22 H6
West Park Road 19 B2
West Place.......................4 F5
West Roedin....................8 G5
West Street......................19 A4
West View 7 D6
West View Terrace 1 B2
West Way Road 20 E5
Western Avenue (Chepstow)
....32 F4
Western Avenue (Newport)
....17 B6
Western Valley Road 17 B5
Westfield 28 F4
Westfield Avenue (Caldicot)
....28 F4

Westfield Avenue (Newport)
....13 D4
Westfield Close 15 C2
Westfield Drive 13 D3
Westfield Road (Caerleon)15 C2
Westfield Road (Newport)..19 A3
Westfield Way 13 D3
Westgate Court 15 D4
Westmoor Close...............21 C5
Weston Villas...................29 B4
Westray Close..................16 G2
Westville Road 19 A2
Westway..........................28 G1
Weyloed Lane 26 E5
Wharf Lane 21 A1
Wharf Road 21 A1
Wheatsheaf Court 27 C4
Wheeler Street 14 G5
Whistler Close..................16 F2
Whitby Mews*, Whitby Pl..14 H6
Whitby Place 14 H6
White Ash Glade 15 D2
White Avenue...................20 H1
White Hart Lane 16 E4
White House Gardens.......6 H6
White Houses...................3 D1
Whitebrook Way...............10 E2
Whitechapel Walk............27 B5
Whitegate House...............3 D3
Whitehall Gardens 27 C5
Whitehall Lane.................10 E4
Whitehouse Close 9 C4
Whitehouse Road.............9 C4
Whitet Houses..................3 B1
Whitethorn Way...............30 H3
Whitewall........................27 C4
Whitstone Road................16 H4
Whittakers Row 7 A4
Whittle Court 13 C3
Whittle Drive 13 C3
Wiesental Close 28 F5
Wilcrick Place 9 B2
Will Paynter Walk*,
    Keir Hardie Drive 16 G6
Willenhall Street...............21 B1
William Brown Close 10 H3
William Lovett Gardens 19 A4
William Morris Drive 16 G6
William Street..................9 C1
Williams Close*, Francis Drive
....19 C5
Willins...........................8 F5
Willow Close (Caldicot)......28 F4
Willow Close (Chepstow)..32 E3
Willow Close (Newport).....21 C4
Willow Close (Rogerstone)
....12 G1
Willow Drive....................23 D5
Willow Green 15 C2
Willows, The (Cwmbran)....9 C3
Willows, The (Redwick)....27 D1
Willows, The (Undy).........27 C4
Wills Row (12) 17 A4
Wilson Road.....................16 G3
Wilson Street...................19 C6
Wimbourne Rise...............7 C5
Winchester Close 19 D3
Windermere Court 7 D5
Windermere Square 16 F1
Windmill Cottages............28 F1
Windmill Lane 28 G1
Windmill Square 19 B6
Windrush Close 14 E1
Windsor Close..................27 C3
Windsor Drive..................27 C3

Windsor Gardens 27 C3
Windsor Park...................27 C3
Windsor Place (13)...........17 A4
Windsor Road (Cwmbran)..8 E5
Windsor Road (Newport)...21 A2
Windsor Road (Pontypool)..6 E2
Windsor Terrace...............19 A4
Wingate Street 19 D5
Winmill Street 19 B6
Winstone House...............2 H3
Winstone Road..................3 D4
Wintour Close..................31 B2
Wirewood Close 31 A5
Wirewood Crescent 31 A5
Wisteria Close 13 C4
Wiston Path 8 F5
Witham Street...................21 A1
Withy Close......................27 C4
Withy Walk......................27 C4
Withyrea Cottages 14 F3
Wolseley Close 19 D6
Wolseley Street 19 D5
Wood Close (Cwmbran)....10 F4
Wood Close (Newport) 12 G3
Wood Crescent 12 G3
Wood Path 9 B3
Wood View*, Coed Cae Pl..4 G4
Woodbine Cottages 4 F1
Woodbine Gardens 27 C4
Woodfield Road.................5 D4
Woodland Court 9 C3
Woodland Drive (Bassaleg)
....17 C3
Woodland Drive (Rogerstone)
....12 F1
Woodland Park Road.........16 H2
Woodland Road (Cwmbran)
....9 C3
Woodland Road (Newport)16 H2
Woodland Road (Underwood)
....23 D5
Woodland Street (Blaenavon)
....1 B4
Woodland Street (Cwmbran)
....7 D6
Woodland Terrace (9)
    (Pontypool)...............3 D2
Woodland Terrace (Varteg).2 E3
Woodland View (Caldicot).28 F4
Woodland View (Garndiffaith)
....2 F1
Woodland View (Pontypool)4 E4
Woodland View (Rogiet) ...28 G2
Woodlands (Talywain)........2 H1
Woodlands Close 31 A1
Woodlands Drive 13 C3
Woodlands Estate 13 C4
Woodlands, The (Pontypool)
....4 E6/5 A1
Woodlands, The *,
    Waterworks Lane....2 H3
Woodley Houses...............1 C6
Woodpecker Close*,
    Barn Owl Road 28 G1
Woods, The 3 D2
Woodside (Newport).........20 F1
Woodside Road (Cwmbran)9 C1
Woodside Road (Pontypool)
....3 C4
Woodside Terrace 9 C1
Woodside Villas................3 C3
Woodside Way 7 C5
Woodside*, Berthon Road ..6 H5
Woodstock Close 28 G4
Woodstock Court 28 G4

Woodstock Way 28 G4
Woodview Court................4 G4
Woodview Terrace*, Albion Rd.
....4 G4
Woodville Road 19 A2
Woolpitch........................7 D4
Worcester Close...............9 D3
Worcester Crescent..........16 F2
Worcester Path 9 D3
Wordsworth Close (Caldicot)
....28 G4
Wordsworth Close (Cwmbran)
....8 E6
Wordsworth Road.............21 A2
Wright Close....................21 C3
Wye Court 7 D4
Wye Crescent (Chepstow)31 D4
Wye Crescent (Newport)...13 D1
Wye Valley Link Road.......32 E2
Wye View Houses*,
    Buttington Road 31 D5
Wyebank Avenue 31 C5
Wyebank Close 31 C5
Wyebank Crescent............31 C5
Wyebank Drive.................31 C5
Wyebank Place.................31 C5
Wyebank Rise 31 C5
Wyebank Road..................31 C5
Wyebank View 31 C5
Wyebank Way 31 D5
Wyecliffe*, Castleford Hill ..31 B4
Wyelands View 32 G1
Wyeverne Road................21 A3
Wyndcliffe Court 31 A1
Wyndcliffe Houses*,
    Buttington Road 31 D5
Wyndcliffe View................31 B1
Wyndham Street 14 H5
Wyngate Street 19 D5
Wyntour Houses*,
    Buttington Road 31 C6
Y
Yellow Row 4 G3
Yeo Close 14 E1
Yetts, The 31 D6
Yew Tree Close (Caldicot)28 G4
Yew Tree Close (Undy).....27 C5
Yew Tree Flats.................10 G1
Yew Tree Lane.................15 D4
Yew Tree Terrace
    (Croesyceiliog)........9 B3
Yew Tree Terrace (Cwmbran)
....10 E1
Yewberry Close................13 D4
Yewberry Lane.................14 E4
Yewtree Cottages 6 E5
Ynys Lane.......................9 B3
York Close.......................7 D4
York Place.......................19 B4
York Road........................16 G1
Ysgol Place......................7 A5
Z
Zion Hill*, Pentrepoid Rd....3 D3

INDUSTRIAL ESTATES
A.R.D. Business Park........5 D3
Abersychan Ind. Estate 3 B3
Albany Trading Estate 14 G5
Avondale Industrial Estate ..9 B2
Boxer Industrial Estate.....15 B3
Bulwark Industrial Estate..32 E4
Cheesemans Ind. Estate ..28 G2
Cleppa Business Park 18 F5
Court Road Ind. Estate.....10 F3
Crawford Trading Estate ..14 G6

Crindau Industrial Estate ...14 F5
Cwmbran Retail Park.........9 D1
Daniel Doncaster Ind. Estate
....1 B2
Docks Way Development Site
....20 E4
Enterprise Park Ind. Estate
....19 C4
Felnex Industrial Estate....22 E2
Forge Hammer Ind. Estate..9 D1
Frederick Street Development
    Site 19 C6
Gilchrist Thomas Ind. Estate
....1 B2
Grange Industrial Estate ...10 E2
Gt. Western Wharf Development
    Site 21 B1
Gwenallt Industrial Estate....4 E1
Herbert Road Ind. Area.....14 G6
Hill Street Ind. Estate........10 F1
Ifton Industrial Estate........28 F2
Ifton Quarry Ind. Estate.....28 G2
Imperial Park 18 G6
Jacks Pill Industrial Estate.19 B6
Johnsey Trading Estate 21 B1
Kay's & Kear's Ind. Estate...1 B2
Langstone Park Business Park
....23 A3
Lee Way Industrial Estate .22 E5
Llandevenny Development Site
....27 C1
Llantarnam Ind. Park...10 H2/H3
Lower Mill Industrial Estate.5 D2
Lyne Road Industrial Area.14 F5
Maesglas Industrial Estate 19 D4
Harlech Retail Park 19 D3
Mill Lane Industrial Estate.31 C4
Mill Parade Ind. Area........19 D6
Mitel Business Park...........29 B1
Mon Bank Sidings Development
    Site 19 C4
Newhouse Farm Ind. Est. .32 H4
Newport Docks Ind. Area ..20 F6
Newport Retail Park 21 D6
North Pontypool Ind. Park...4 E3
Old Town Dock Development
....21 C1
Oldbury Business Centre ..10 E1
Panteg Industrial Estate 6 E2
Pavilion Indusrtial Estate....3 D4
Pill Farm Industrial Estate .29 D1
Polo Grounds Ind. Estate...5 D3
Pontnewydd Bus. Centre ...4 E2
Pontnewydd Ind. Estate 4 E2
Pontyfelin Industrial Estate.6 E3
Queensway Meadows Ind. Est.
....21 D5
Reevesland Ind. Estate 22 E3
School Hill Trading Estate.31 C4
Severn Bridge Ind. Estate .29 C1
Somerset Industrial Estate..9 C2
South Pontypool Ind. Park ..5 D3
Springvale Industrial Estate 7 C5
Star Trading Estate 15 B3
Station Yard Ind. Estate 31 C4
Stephenson St. Ind. Est. ...22 E1
Torfaen Business Centre ...5 D3
Transporter Bridge Development
    Site 21 D1
Traverner Trading Estate ..15 D4
Tregwilym Industrial Estate
....17 B4
Ty Coch Industrial Estate ..10 F1
Wern Industrial Estate.......12 H3
Western Industrial Estate..15 C4

ORDER FORM

A series of Streetezee atlases is being developed in Wales and England. The maps are based on the Ordnance Survey and are revised and updated regularly.

All the titles are available from bookshops, motorway service stations, newsagents, supermarkets and petrol stations, or by mail order direct from the publisher. Trade enquiries welcome.

Simply complete the order form (it may be photocopied) and post it to: Streetezee Town Plans Ltd. The Lydart, Monmouth, NP25 4RJ; or phone/fax direct on 01600 719000.

ISBN	Title	Price	Quantity	Total
1-902884-16-7	Barry	£1.95		
1-902884-04-3	Bridgend	£2.50		
1-902884-20-5	Cardiff	£3.50		
1-902884-22-1	Cardiff - Mega Atlas	£4.75		
1-902884-14-0	Flintshire	£2.75		
1-902884-15-9	Hereford & Monmouth	£2.25		
1-902884-13-2	Llandudno	£2.75		
1-902884-02-7	Llanelli	£2.25		
1-902884-17-5	Mid Wales	£2.95		
1-902884-01-9	Neath	£2.25		
1-902884-21-3	Newport	£3.50		
1-902884-11-6	North West Wales	£2.95		
1-902884-00-0	Port Talbot	£2.25		
1-902884-18-3	Shrewsbury & W. Shropshire	£2.50		
1-902884-03-5	Swansea	£2.95		
1-902884-19-1	Telford & E. Shropshire	£2.95		
1-902884-12-4	Valleys-East	£3.25		
1-902884-08-6	Valleys-West	£3.25		
1-902884-07-8	West Wales	£3.25		

Name..

Street..

Town..

County.......................................

Post Code..................................

I enclose a cheque/postal order for the value of ....
made payable to Streetezee Town Plans Ltd.

Signature..................................

Date...